APPALACHIAN TRAIL

Book of Profiles

APPALACHIAN TRAIL

Book of Profiles

APPALACHIAN TRAIL
CONSERVANCY

Harpers Ferry

Cover: Hiker crossing Franconia Ridge, White Mountain National Forest, New Hampshire. © 2013 Valerie A. Long

Elevation profiles prepared by Mapping Specialists, Ltd., Fitchburg, Wis.; derived primarily from the 2012 *Appalachian Trail Data Book* and geographical-information-system resources of the Appalachian Trail Conservancy. Because of the ever-changing nature of the footpath route, some minor deviations should be expected between these representations and the actual distances between points in a given month. Vertical exaggeration: 5.28.

First edition

ISBN 978-1-889386-87-4

Contents

Key to Symbols

In addition to the conventional icons for federal, state, and local highways, the profiles use these icons:

P parking

▣ water

◣ shelter

▲ campsite (not all are indicated; see guidebooks)

GEORGIA

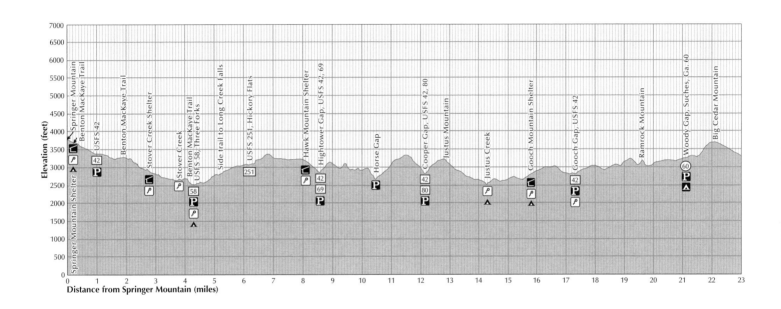

Elevation (feet)

7000
6500
6000
5500
5000
4500
4000
3500
3000
2500
2000
1500
1000
500
0

Distance from Springer Mountain (miles)

0 1 2 3 4 5 6 7 8 9 10 11 12 13 14 15 16 17 18 19 20 21 22 23

Springer Mountain
Benton MacKaye Trail
USFS 42
Benton MacKaye Trail
Stover Creek Shelter
Stover Creek
Benton MacKaye Trail
USFS 58, Three Forks
Side trail to Long Creek Falls
USFS 251, Hickory Flats
Hawk Mountain Shelter
Hightower Gap, USFS 42, 69
Horse Gap
Cooper Gap, USFS 42, 80
Justus Mountain
Justus Creek
Gooch Mountain Shelter
Gooch Gap, USFS 42
Ramrock Mountain
Woody Gap, Suches, Ga. 60
Big Cedar Mountain

Springer Mountain Shelter

Appalachian Trail Guide to North Carolina–Georgia →

GEORGIA

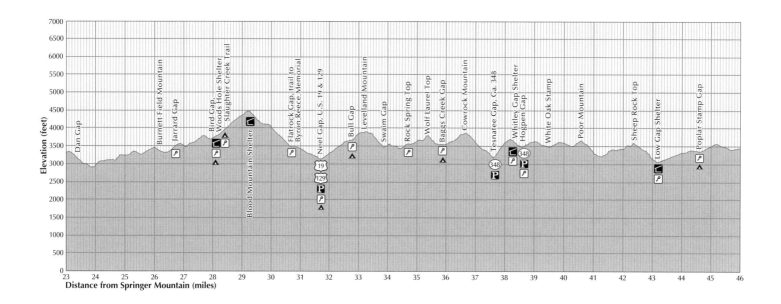

Elevation (feet)

Distance from Springer Mountain (miles)

Dan Gap
Burnett Field Mountain
Jarrard Gap
Bird Gap, Woods Hole Shelter
Slaughter Creek Trail
Blood Mountain Shelter
Flatrock Gap, trail to Byron Reece Memorial
Neel Gap, U.S. 19 & 129
Bull Gap
Levelland Mountain
Swaim Gap
Rock Spring Top
Wolf Laurel Top
Baggs Creek Gap
Cowrock Mountain
Tesnatee Gap, Ga. 348
Whitley Gap Shelter
Hogpen Gap
White Oak Stamp
Poor Mountain
Sheep Rock Top
Low Gap Shelter
Poplar Stamp Gap

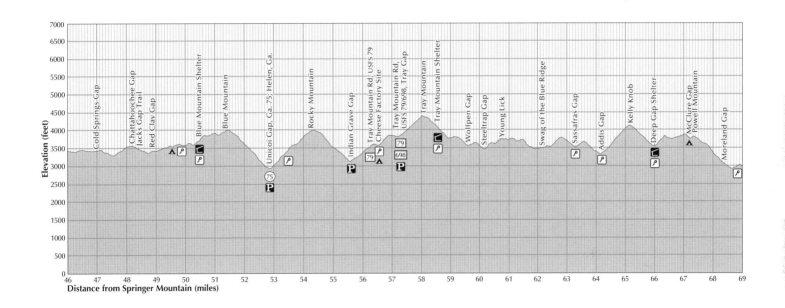

Elevation (feet)

7000
6500
6000
5500
5000
4500
4000
3500
3000
2500
2000
1500
1000
500
0

Cold Springs Gap
Chattahoochee Gap
Jacks Gap Trail
Red Clay Gap
Blue Mountain Shelter
Blue Mountain
Unicoi Gap, Ga.-75; Helen, Ga.
Rocky Mountain
Indian Grave Gap
Tray Mountain Rd, USFS 79
Cheese Factory Site
Tray Mountain Rd, USFS 79/698, Tray Gap
Tray Mountain
Tray Mountain Shelter
Wolfpen Gap
Steeltrap Gap
Young Lick
Swag of the Blue Ridge
Sassafras Gap
Addis Gap
Kelly Knob
Deep Gap Shelter
McClure Gap
Powell Mountain
Moreland Gap

75
79
698
79

Distance from Springer Mountain (miles)

46 47 48 49 50 51 52 53 54 55 56 57 58 59 60 61 62 63 64 65 66 67 68 69

Appalachian Trail Book of Profiles

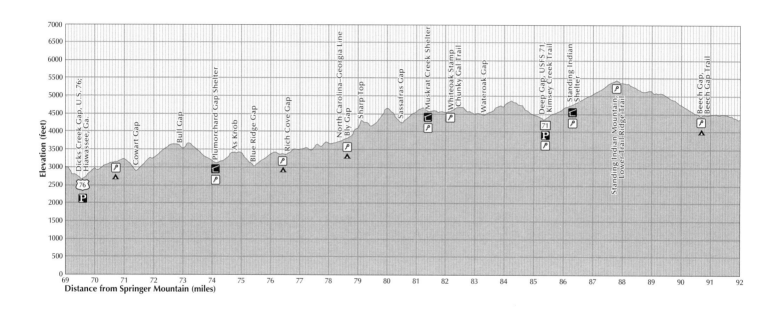

Elevation (feet)

Distance from Springer Mountain (miles)

- Dicks Creek Gap, U.S. 76; Hiawassee, Ga.
- Cowart Gap
- Bull Gap
- Plumorchard Gap Shelter
- As Knob
- Blue Ridge Gap
- Rich Cove Gap
- North Carolina–Georgia Line
- Bly Gap
- Sharp Top
- Sassafras Gap
- Muskrat Creek Shelter
- Whiteoak Stamp
- Chunky Gal Trail
- Wateroak Gap
- Deep Gap, USFS 71
- Kimsey Creek Trail
- Standing Indian Shelter
- Standing Indian Mountain; Lower Trail Ridge Trail
- Beech Gap; Beech Gap Trail

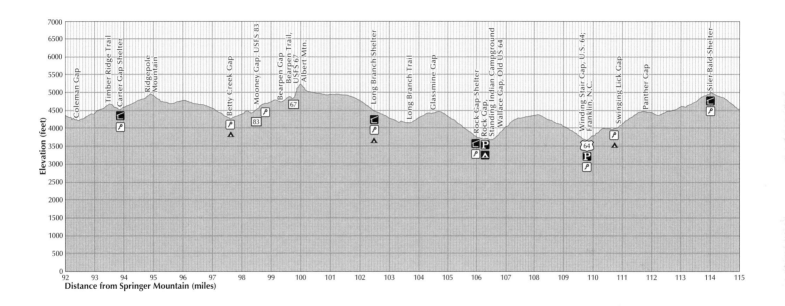

Elevation (feet)

Distance from Springer Mountain (miles)

Coleman Gap
Timber Ridge Trail
Carter Gap Shelter
Ridgepole Mountain
Betty Creek Gap
Mooney Gap, USFS 83
83
Bearpen Gap
Bearpen Trail, USFS 67
67
Albert Mtn.
Long Branch Shelter
Long Branch Trail
Glassmine Gap
Rock Gap Shelter
Rock Gap, Standing Indian Campground
Wallace Gap, Old US 64
Winding Stair Gap, U.S. 64; Franklin, N.C.
64
Swinging Lick Gap
Panther Gap
Siler Bald Shelter

NORTH CAROLINA

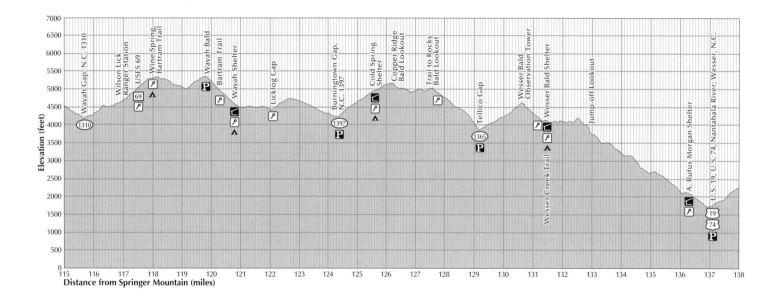

Distance from Springer Mountain (miles)

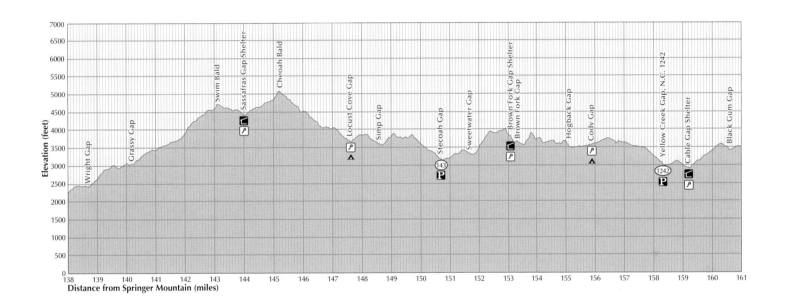

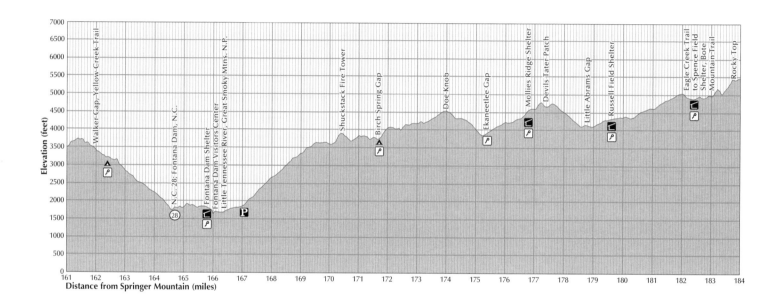

Appalachian Trail Book of Profiles

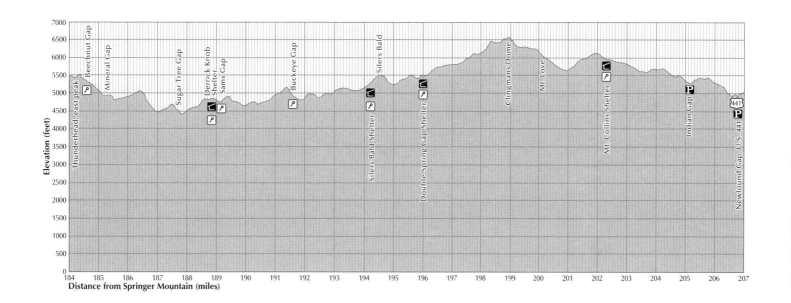

Elevation (feet)

7000
6500
6000
5500
5000
4500
4000
3500
3000
2500
2000
1500
1000
500
0

184 185 186 187 188 189 190 191 192 193 194 195 196 197 198 199 200 201 202 203 204 205 206 207

Distance from Springer Mountain (miles)

Thunderhead, east peak
Beechnut Gap
Mineral Gap
Sugar Tree Gap
Derrick Knob Shelter
Sams Gap
Buckeye Gap
Silers Bald
Silers Bald Shelter
Double Spring Gap Shelter
Clingmans Dome
Mt. Love
Mt. Collins Shelter
Indian Gap
Newfound Gap, U.S. 441
441

Appalachian Trail Guide to Tennessee–North Carolina →

NORTH CAROLINA—TENNESSEE BORDER

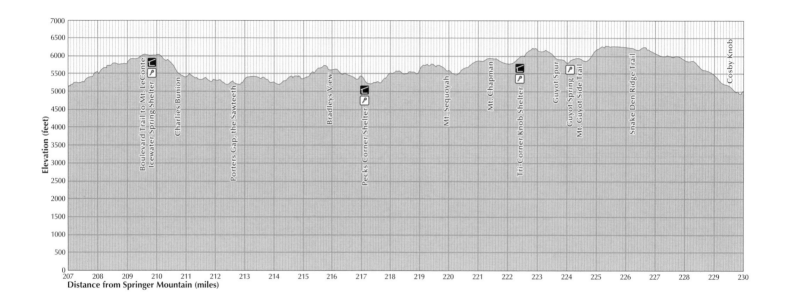

Elevation (feet) / Distance from Springer Mountain (miles)

- Boulevard Trail to Mt. LeConte
- Icewater Spring Shelter
- Charlies Bunion
- Porters Gap, the Sawteeth
- Bradleys View
- Pecks Corner Shelter
- Mt. Sequoyah
- Mt. Chapman
- Tri-Corner Knob Shelter
- Guyot Spur
- Guyot Spring
- Mt. Guyot Side Trail
- Snake Den Ridge Trail
- Cosby Knob

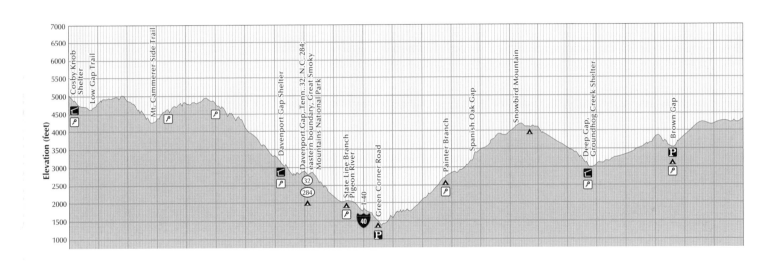

Elevation (feet)

Cosby Knob Shelter
Low Gap Trail
Mt. Cammerer Side Trail
Davenport Gap Shelter
Davenport Gap, Tenn. 32; N.C. 284; eastern boundary, Great Smoky Mountains National Park
State Line Branch Pigeon River
32
284
I-40
Green Corner Road
40
Painter Branch
Spanish Oak Gap
Snowbird Mountain
Deep Gap, Groundhog Creek Shelter
Brown Gap

7000
6500
6000
5500
5000
4500
4000
3500
3000
2500
2000
1500
1000

Appalachian Trail Book of Profiles

NORTH CAROLINA

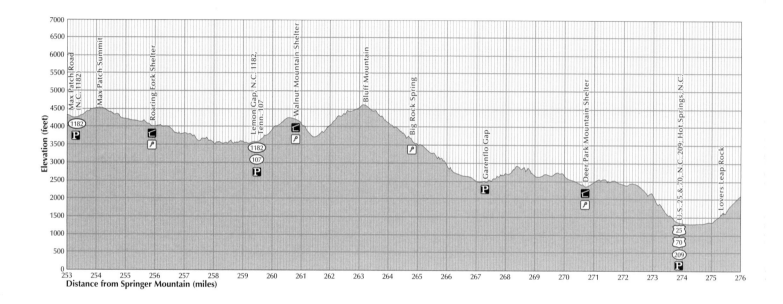

Elevation (feet) — vertical axis: 0, 500, 1000, 1500, 2000, 2500, 3000, 3500, 4000, 4500, 5000, 5500, 6000, 6500, 7000

Distance from Springer Mountain (miles) — horizontal axis: 253, 254, 255, 256, 257, 258, 259, 260, 261, 262, 263, 264, 265, 266, 267, 268, 269, 270, 271, 272, 273, 274, 275, 276

Labels:
- Max Patch Road (N.C. 1182)
- Max Patch Summit
- Roaring Fork Shelter
- Lemon Gap, N.C. 1182; Tenn. 107
- Walnut Mountain Shelter
- Bluff Mountain
- Big Rock Spring
- Garenflo Gap
- Deer Park Mountain Shelter
- U.S. 25 & 70, N.C. 209; Hot Springs, N.C.
- Lovers Leap Rock

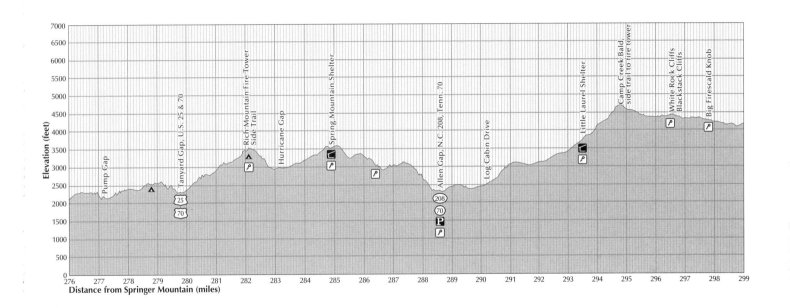

Elevation (feet)

Distance from Springer Mountain (miles)

Pump Gap

Tanyard Gap, U.S. 25 & 70

Rich Mountain Fire Tower Side Trail

Hurricane Gap

Spring Mountain Shelter

Allen Gap, N.C. 208, Tenn. 70

Log Cabin Drive

Little Laurel Shelter

Camp Creek Bald side trail to fire tower

White Rock Cliffs
Blackstack Cliffs

Big Firescald Knob

NORTH CAROLINA–TENNESSEE BORDER

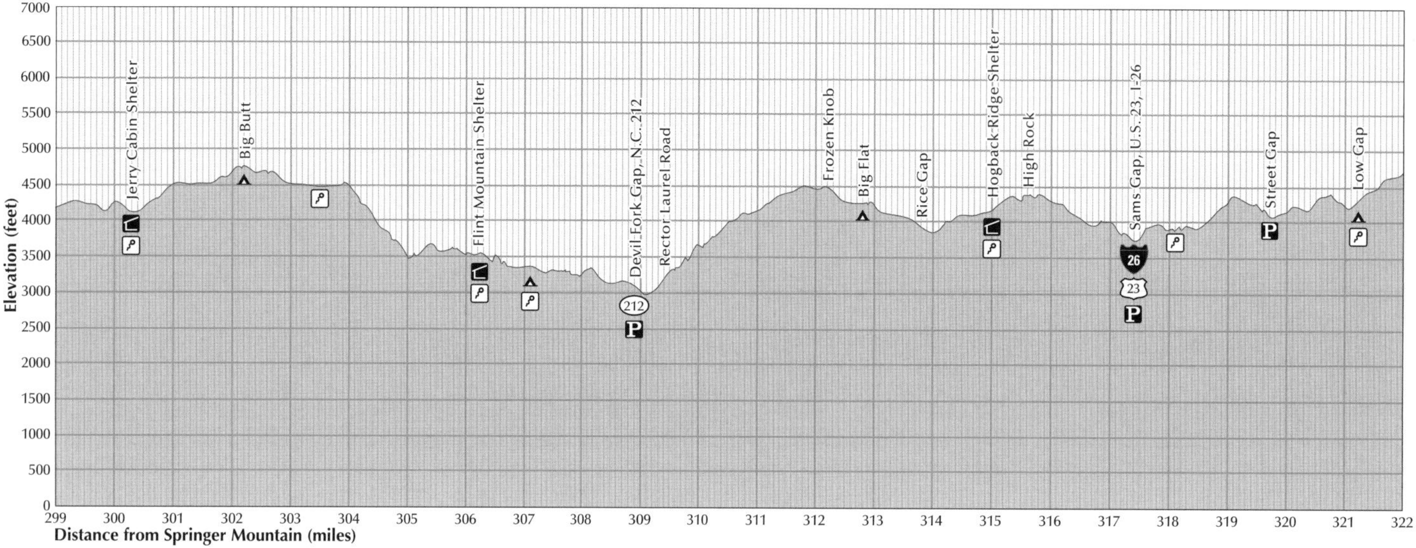
Elevation (feet)
7000
6500
6000
5500
5000
4500
4000
3500
3000
2500
2000
1500
1000
500
0
Jerry Cabin Shelter
Big Butt
Flint Mountain Shelter
Devil Fork Gap, N.C. 212
Rector Laurel Road
Frozen Knob
Big Flat
Rice Gap
Hogback Ridge Shelter
High Rock
Sams Gap, U.S. 23, I-26
Street Gap
Low Gap
212
26
23
299
300
301
302
303
304
305
306
307
308
309
310
311
312
313
314
315
316
317
318
319
320
321
322
Distance from Springer Mountain (miles)

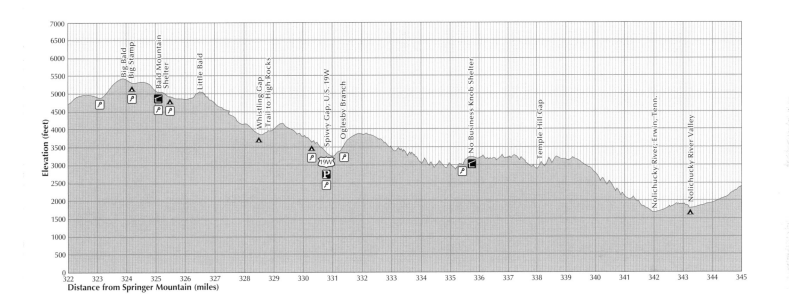

Elevation (feet)

Distance from Springer Mountain (miles)

Labels on profile (left to right): Big Bald, Big Stamp, Bald Mountain Shelter, Little Bald, Whistling Gap, Trail to High Rocks, Spivey Gap, U.S. 19W, Oglesby Branch, 19W, No Business Knob Shelter, Temple Hill Gap, Nolichucky River; Erwin, Tenn., Nolichucky River Valley

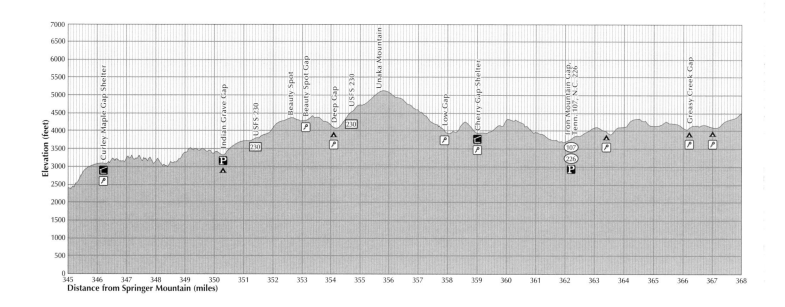

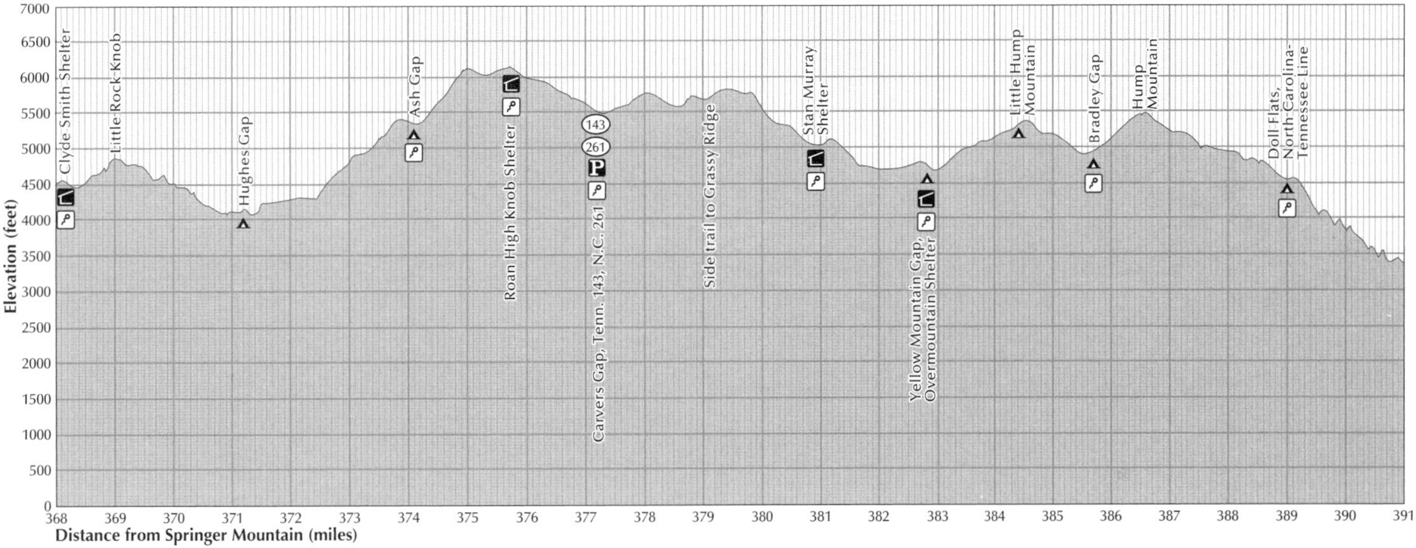
Elevation (feet)
7000
6500
6000
5500
5000
4500
4000
3500
3000
2500
2000
1500
1000
500
0
Clyde Smith Shelter
Little Rock Knob
Hughes Gap
Ash Gap
Roan High Knob Shelter
143
261
Carvers Gap, Tenn. 143, N.C. 261
Side trail to Grassy Ridge
Stan Murray Shelter
Yellow Mountain Gap, Overmountain Shelter
Little Hump Mountain
Bradley Gap
Hump Mountain
Doll Flats, North Carolina-Tennessee Line
368
369
370
371
372
373
374
375
376
377
378
379
380
381
382
383
384
385
386
387
388
389
390
391
Distance from Springer Mountain (miles)

TENNESSEE

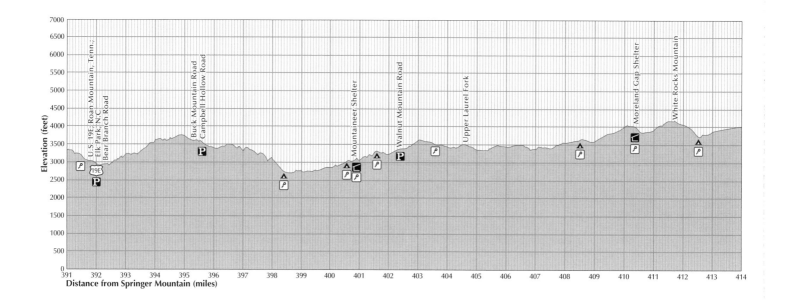

Elevation (feet)

7000
6500
6000
5500
5000
4500
4000
3500
3000
2500
2000
1500
1000
500
0

Distance from Springer Mountain (miles)

391 392 393 394 395 396 397 398 399 400 401 402 403 404 405 406 407 408 409 410 411 412 413 414

U.S. 19E; Roan Mountain, Tenn.; Elk Park, N.C.
Bear Branch Road
Buck Mountain Road
Campbell Hollow Road
Mountaineer Shelter
Walnut Mountain Road
Upper Laurel Fork
Moreland Gap Shelter
White Rocks Mountain

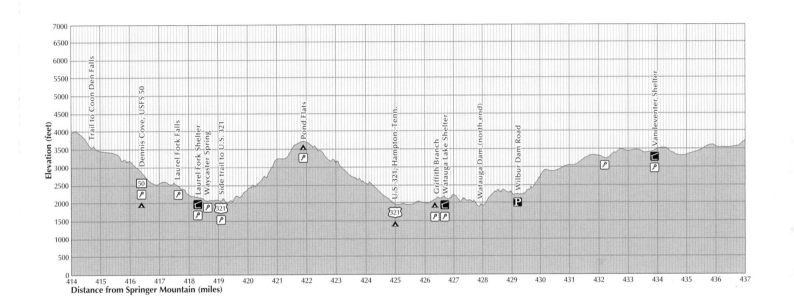

Elevation (feet)

7000
6500
6000
5500
5000
4500
4000
3500
3000
2500
2000
1500
1000
500
0

Trail to Coon Den Falls

Dennis Cove, USFS 50

50

Laurel Fork Falls

Laurel Fork Shelter
Waycaster Spring

321

Side trail to U.S. 321

Pond Flats

U.S. 321, Hampton, Tenn.

321

Griffith Branch
Watauga Lake Shelter

Watauga Dam (north end)

Wilbur Dam Road

P

Vandeventer Shelter

Distance from Springer Mountain (miles)

414 415 416 417 418 419 420 421 422 423 424 425 426 427 428 429 430 431 432 433 434 435 436 437

Appalachian Trail Book of Profiles

TENNESSEE

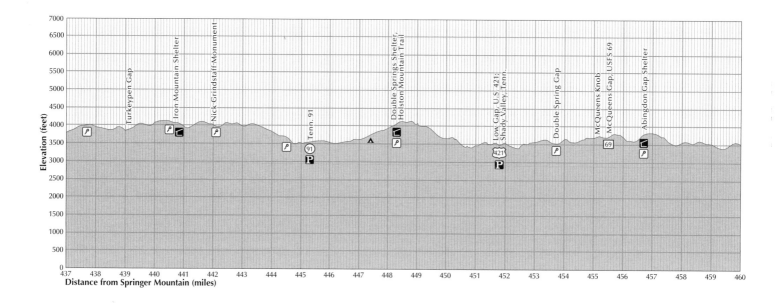

Elevation (feet)

7000
6500
6000
5500
5000
4500
4000
3500
3000
2500
2000
1500
1000
500
0

Turkeypen Gap
Iron Mountain Shelter
Nick Grindstaff Monument
Tenn. 91
Double Springs Shelter; Holston Mountain Trail
Low Gap, U.S. 421; Shady Valley, Tenn.
Double Spring Gap
McQueens Knob
McQueens Gap, USFS 69
Abingdon Gap Shelter

437 438 439 440 441 442 443 444 445 446 447 448 449 450 451 452 453 454 455 456 457 458 459 460

Distance from Springer Mountain (miles)

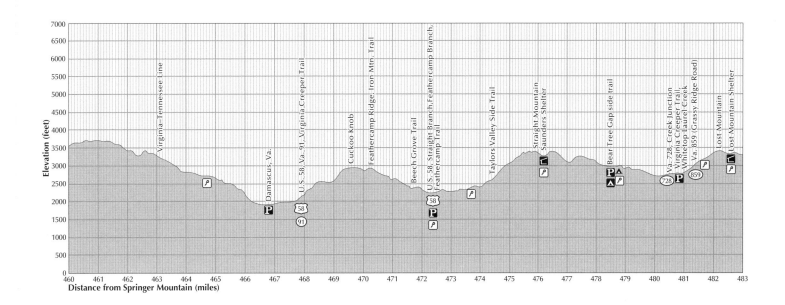

Appalachian Trail Guide to Southwest Virginia →

VIRGINIA

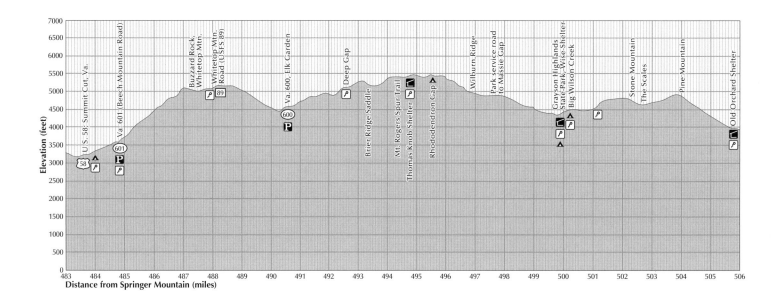

Elevation (feet)

Distance from Springer Mountain (miles)

U.S. 58; Summit Cut, Va.

Va. 601 (Beech Mountain Road)

Buzzard Rock, Whitetop Mtn.

Whitetop Mtn. Road (USFS 89)

Va. 600, Elk Garden

Deep Gap

Brier Ridge Saddle

Mt. Rogers Spur Trail

Thomas Knob Shelter

Rhododendron Gap

Wilburn Ridge

Park service road to Massie Gap

Grayson Highlands State Park; Wise Shelter

Big Wilson Creek

Stone Mountain

The Scales

Pine Mountain

Old Orchard Shelter

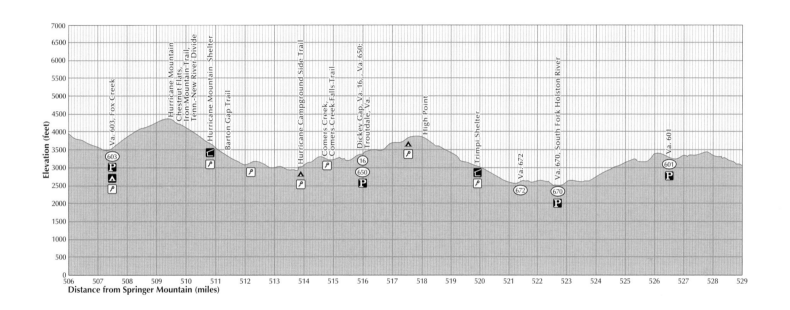

Elevation (feet)

7000
6500
6000
5500
5000
4500
4000
3500
3000
2500
2000
1500
1000
500
0

Va. 603, Fox Creek

Hurricane Mountain
Chestnut Flats,
Iron-Mountain Trail;
Tenn.–New River Divide

Hurricane Mountain Shelter

Barton Gap Trail

Hurricane Campground Side Trail

Comers Creek;
Comers-Creek-Falls Trail

Dickey Gap, Va. 16, Va. 650;
Troutdale, Va.

High Point

Trimpi Shelter

Va. 672

Va. 670, South Fork Holston River

Va. 601

603
P
Δ

411
P
P
Δ
P
16
650
P

Δ
P

411
P
672
670
P

601
P

506 507 508 509 510 511 512 513 514 515 516 517 518 519 520 521 522 523 524 525 526 527 528 529

Distance from Springer Mountain (miles)

VIRGINIA

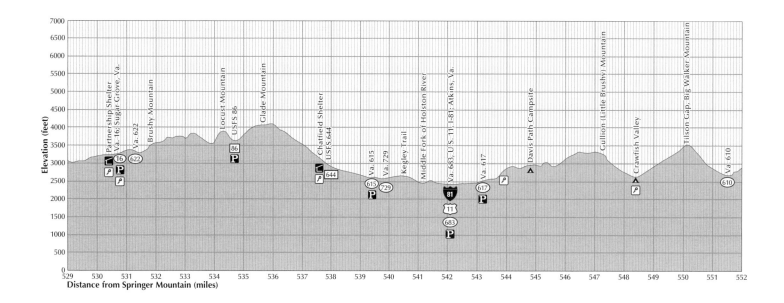

Elevation (feet)

Distance from Springer Mountain (miles)

Labels on profile (left to right):
- Partnership Shelter
- Va. 16; Sugar Grove, Va.
- Va. 622
- Brushy Mountain
- Locust Mountain
- USFS 86
- Glade Mountain
- Chatfield Shelter
- USFS 644
- Va. 615
- Va. 729
- Kegley Trail
- Middle Fork of Holston River
- Va. 683, U.S. 11, I-81; Atkins, Va.
- Va. 617
- Davis Path Campsite
- Gullion (Little Brushy) Mountain
- Crawfish Valley
- Tilson Gap; Big Walker Mountain
- Va. 610

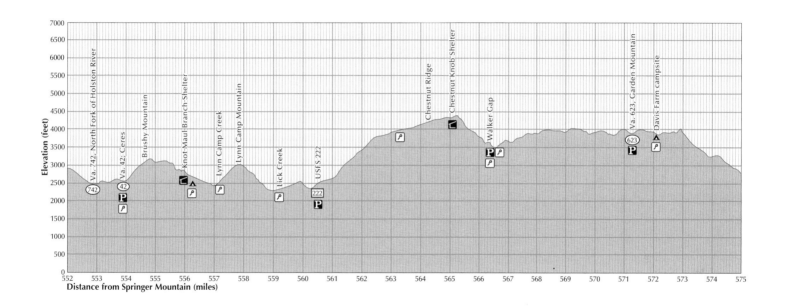

Elevation (feet)

Distance from Springer Mountain (miles)

Va. 742, North Fork of Holston River

Va. 42, Ceres

Brushy Mountain

Knot Maul Branch Shelter

Lynn Camp Creek

Lynn Camp Mountain

Lick Creek

USFS 222

Chestnut Ridge

Chestnut Knob Shelter

Walker Gap

Va. 623, Garden Mountain

Davis Farm campsite

VIRGINIA

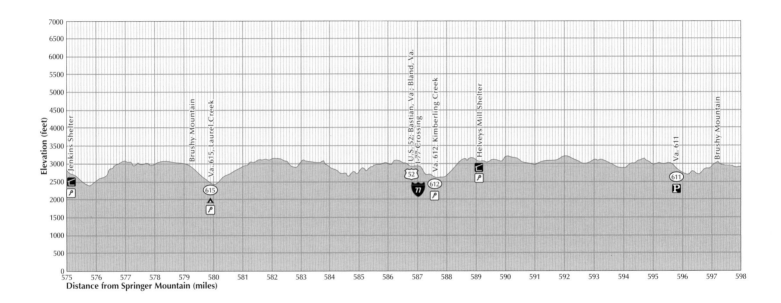

Elevation (feet)

Distance from Springer Mountain (miles)

Jenkins Shelter

Brushy Mountain

Va. 615, Laurel Creek

U.S. 52; Bastian, Va.; Bland, Va.
I-77 Crossing

Va. 612, Kimberling Creek

Helveys Mill Shelter

Va. 611

Brushy Mountain

Appalachian Trail Book of Profiles

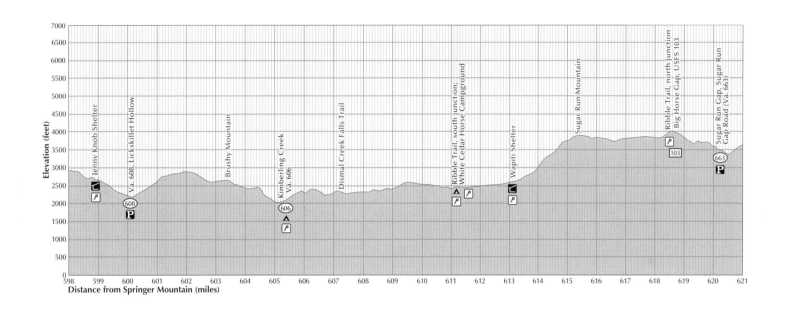

Elevation (feet)

7000
6500
6000
5500
5000
4500
4000
3500
3000
2500
2000
1500
1000
500
0

Jenny Knob Shelter
Va. 608, Lickskillet Hollow
Brushy Mountain
Kimberling Creek
Va. 606
Dismal Creek Falls Trail
Ribble Trail, south junction;
White Cedar Horse Campground
Wapiti Shelter
Sugar Run Mountain
Ribble Trail, north junction
Big Horse Gap, USFS 103
Sugar Run Gap, Sugar Run
Gap Road (Va. 663)

608
606
103
663

Distance from Springer Mountain (miles)

598 599 600 601 602 603 604 605 606 607 608 609 610 611 612 613 614 615 616 617 618 619 620 621

Appalachian Trail Book of Profiles

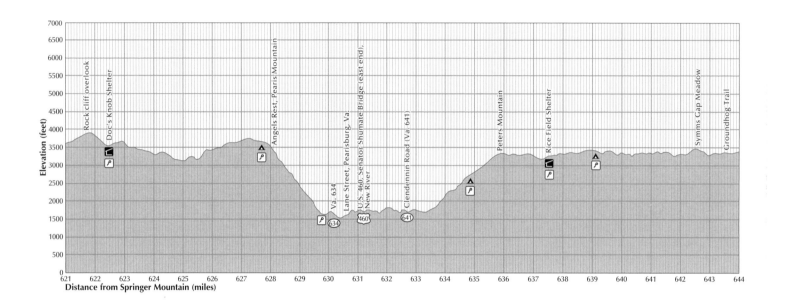

Appalachian Trail Guide to Central Virginia →

Appalachian Trail Book of Profiles

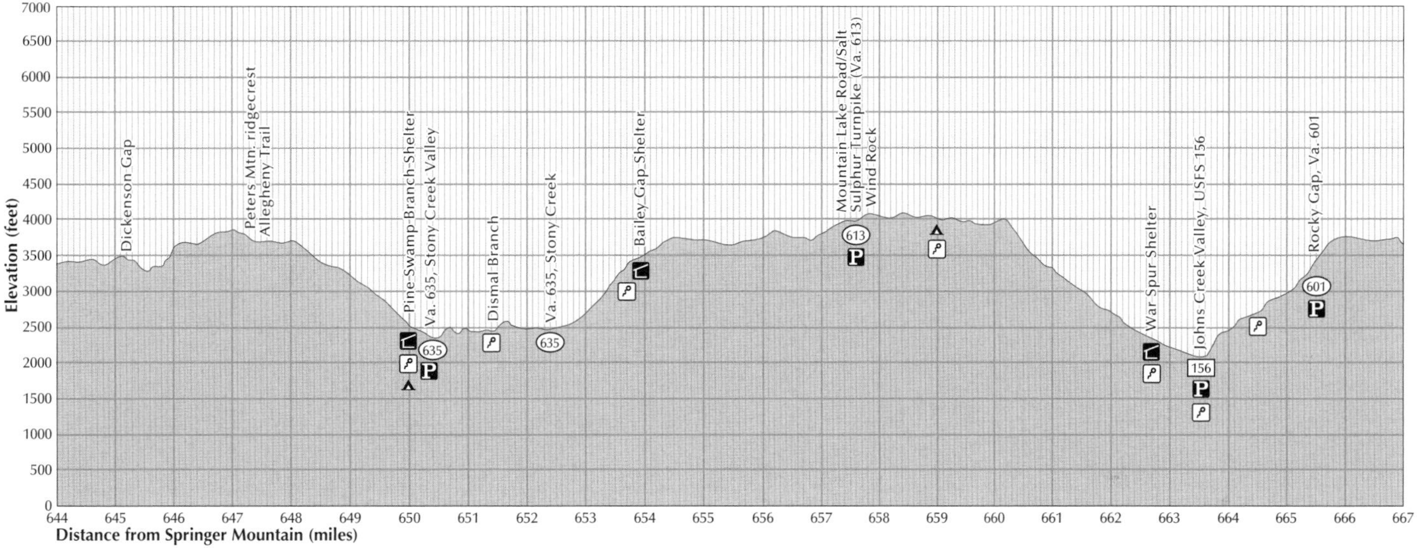
Dickenson Gap
Peters Mtn. ridgecrest
Allegheny Trail
Pine Swamp Branch Shelter
Va. 635, Stony Creek Valley
Dismal Branch
Va. 635, Stony Creek
Bailey Gap Shelter
Mountain Lake Road/Salt
Sulphur Turnpike (Va. 613)
Wind Rock
War Spur Shelter
Johns Creek Valley, USFS 156
Rocky Gap, Va. 601
635
635
613
156
601
Elevation (feet)
7000
6500
6000
5500
5000
4500
4000
3500
3000
2500
2000
1500
1000
500
0
644
645
646
647
648
649
650
651
652
653
654
655
656
657
658
659
660
661
662
663
664
665
666
667
Distance from Springer Mountain (miles)

VIRGINIA

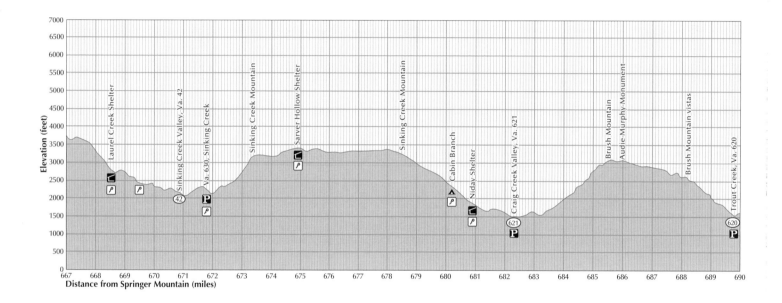

Elevation (feet)

7000
6500
6000
5500
5000
4500
4000
3500
3000
2500
2000
1500
1000
500
0

Laurel Creek Shelter
Sinking Creek Valley, Va. 42
Va. 630, Sinking Creek
Sinking Creek Mountain
Sarver Hollow Shelter
Sinking Creek Mountain
Cabin Branch
Niday Shelter
Craig Creek Valley, Va. 621
Brush Mountain
Audie-Murphy-Monument
Brush Mountain vistas
Trout Creek, Va. 620

667 668 669 670 671 672 673 674 675 676 677 678 679 680 681 682 683 684 685 686 687 688 689 690

Distance from Springer Mountain (miles)

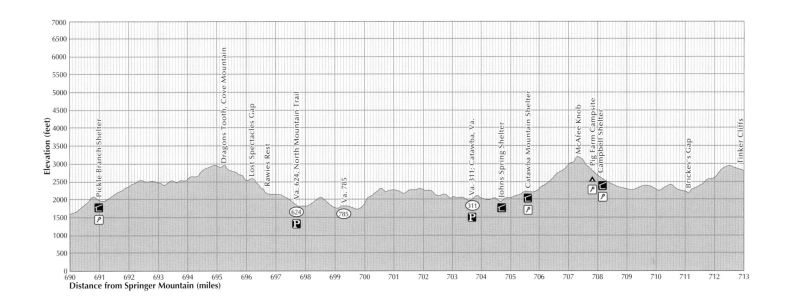

Distance from Springer Mountain (miles)

Elevation (feet)

Pickle Branch Shelter

Dragons Tooth, Cove Mountain

Lost Spectacles Gap

Rawies Rest

Va. 624, North Mountain Trail

Va. 785

Va. 311; Catawba, Va.

Johns Spring Shelter

Catawba Mountain Shelter

McAfee Knob

Pig Farm Campsite

Campbell Shelter

Brickey's Gap

Tinker Cliffs

VIRGINIA

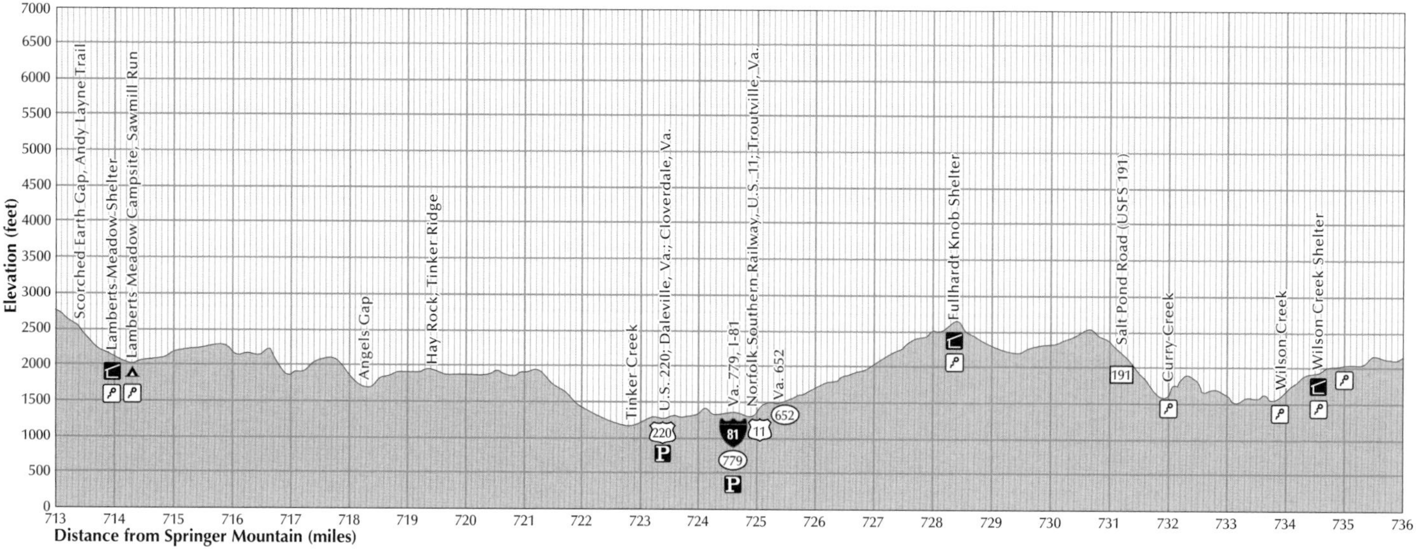

Elevation (feet)
7000
6500
6000
5500
5000
4500
4000
3500
3000
2500
2000
1500
1000
500
0
Scorched Earth Gap, Andy Layne Trail
Lamberts Meadow Shelter
Lamberts Meadow Campsite, Sawmill Run
Angels Gap
Hay Rock, Tinker Ridge
Tinker Creek
U.S. 220; Daleville, Va.; Cloverdale, Va.
Va. 779, I-81
Norfolk Southern Railway, U.S. 11; Troutville, Va.
Va. 652
Fullhardt Knob Shelter
Salt Pond Road (USFS 191)
Curry Creek
Wilson Creek
Wilson Creek Shelter
220
P
81
11
779
P
652
191
713
714
715
716
717
718
719
720
721
722
723
724
725
726
727
728
729
730
731
732
733
734
735
736
Distance from Springer Mountain (miles)

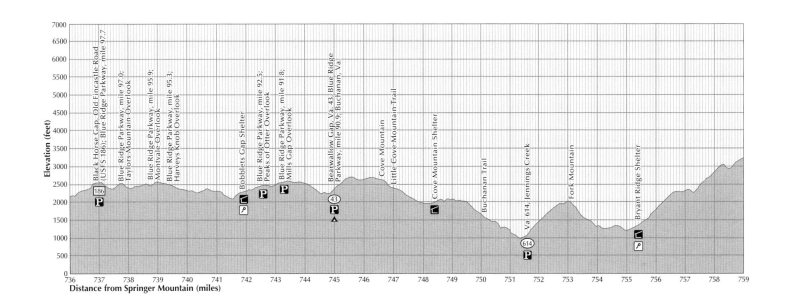

Elevation (feet)

7000
6500
6000
5500
5000
4500
4000
3500
3000
2500
2000
1500
1000
500
0

Black Horse Gap, Old Fincastle Road (USFS 186); Blue Ridge Parkway, mile 97.7

186

Blue Ridge Parkway, mile 97.0; Taylors Mountain Overlook

Blue Ridge Parkway, mile 95.9; Montvale Overlook

Blue Ridge Parkway, mile 95.3; Harveys Knob Overlook

Bobblets Gap Shelter

Blue Ridge Parkway, mile 92.5; Peaks of Otter Overlook

Blue Ridge Parkway, mile 91.8; Mills Gap Overlook

Bearwallow Gap, Va. 43; Blue Ridge Parkway, mile 90.9; Buchanan, Va.

43

Cove Mountain

Little Cove Mountain Trail

Cove Mountain Shelter

Buchanan Trail

Va. 614, Jennings Creek

614

Fork Mountain

Bryant Ridge Shelter

Distance from Springer Mountain (miles)

736 737 738 739 740 741 742 743 744 745 746 747 748 749 750 751 752 753 754 755 756 757 758 759

VIRGINIA

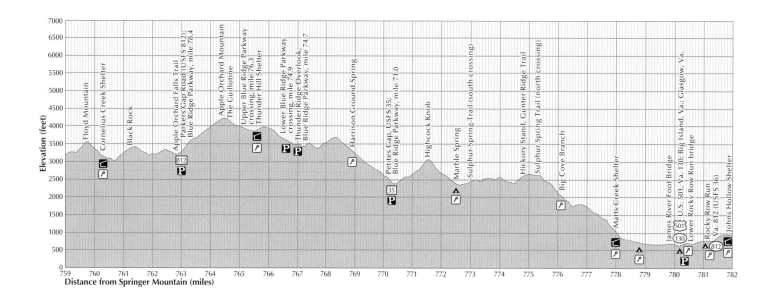

Elevation (feet)

Distance from Springer Mountain (miles)

Floyd Mountain
Cornelius Creek Shelter
Black Rock
Apple Orchard Falls Trail
Parkers Gap Road (USFS 812);
Blue Ridge Parkway, mile 78.4
Apple Orchard Mountain
The Guillotine
Upper Blue Ridge Parkway
crossing, mile 76.3
Thunder Hill Shelter
Lower Blue Ridge Parkway
crossing, mile 74.9
Thunder Ridge Overlook;
Blue Ridge Parkway, mile 74.7
Harrison Ground Spring
Petites Gap, USFS 35;
Blue Ridge Parkway, mile 71.0
Highcock Knob
Marble Spring
Sulphur Spring Trail (south crossing)
Hickory Stand, Gunter Ridge Trail
Sulphur Spring Trail (north crossing)
Big Cove Branch
Matts Creek Shelter
James River Foot Bridge
U.S. 501, Va. 130; Big Island, Va.; Glasgow, Va.
Lower Rocky Row Run bridge
Rocky Row Run
Va. 812 (USFS 36)
Johns Hollow Shelter

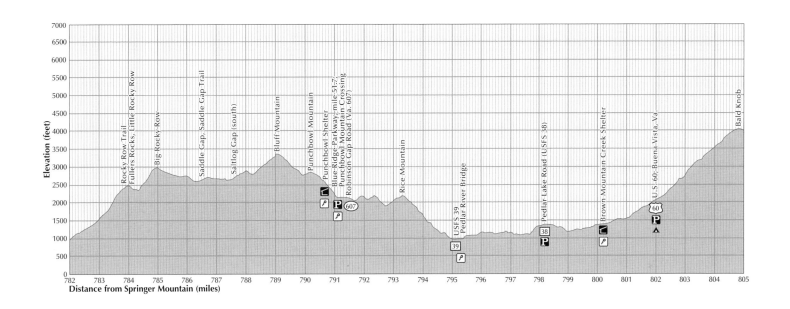

Elevation (feet)

7000
6500
6000
5500
5000
4500
4000
3500
3000
2500
2000
1500
1000
500
0

Rocky Row Trail
Fullers Rocks, Little Rocky Row
Big Rocky Row
Saddle Gap, Saddle Gap Trail
Saltlog Gap (south)
Bluff Mountain
Punchbowl Mountain
Punchbowl Shelter
Blue Ridge Parkway, mile 51.7
Punchbowl Mountain Crossing
Robinson Gap Road (Va. 607)
Rice Mountain
USFS 39
Pedlar River Bridge
Pedlar Lake Road (USFS 38)
Brown Mountain Creek Shelter
U.S. 60; Buena Vista, Va.
Bald Knob

607
39
38
60

Distance from Springer Mountain (miles)

782 783 784 785 786 787 788 789 790 791 792 793 794 795 796 797 798 799 800 801 802 803 804 805

VIRGINIA

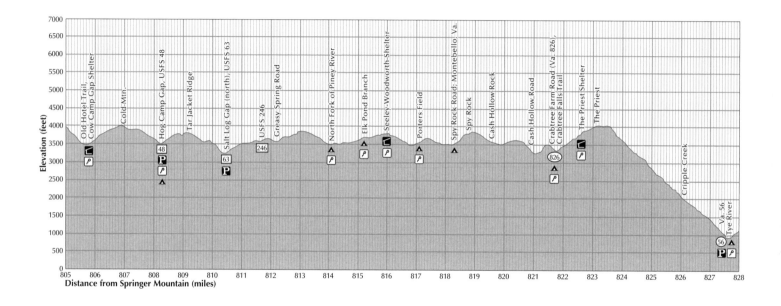

Elevation (feet) — vertical axis: 0, 500, 1000, 1500, 2000, 2500, 3000, 3500, 4000, 4500, 5000, 5500, 6000, 6500, 7000

Distance from Springer Mountain (miles) — horizontal axis: 805, 806, 807, 808, 809, 810, 811, 812, 813, 814, 815, 816, 817, 818, 819, 820, 821, 822, 823, 824, 825, 826, 827, 828

Labels along the profile:
- Old Hotel Trail, Cow Camp Gap Shelter
- Cold Mtn.
- Hog Camp Gap, USFS 48
- Tar Jacket Ridge
- Salt Log Gap (north), USFS 63
- USFS 246
- Greasy Spring Road
- North Fork of Piney River
- Elk Pond Branch
- Seeley-Woodworth Shelter
- Porters Field
- Spy Rock Road; Montebello, Va.
- Spy Rock
- Cash Hollow Rock
- Cash Hollow Road
- Crabtree Farm Road (Va. 826), Crabtree Falls Trail
- The Priest Shelter
- The Priest
- Cripple Creek
- Va. 56
- Tye River

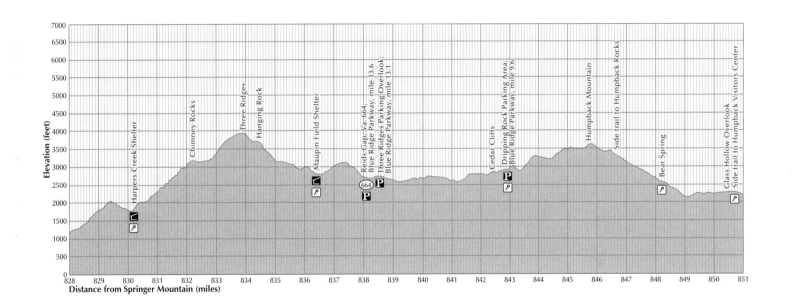

Elevation (feet)

Harpers Creek Shelter

Chimney Rocks

Three Ridges

Hanging Rock

Maupin Field Shelter

Reids Gap, Va-664; Blue Ridge Parkway, mile 13.6

Three Ridges Parking Overlook; Blue Ridge Parkway, mile 13.1

Cedar Cliffs

Dripping Rock Parking Area; Blue Ridge Parkway, mile 9.6

Humpback Mountain

Side trail to Humpback Rocks

Bear Spring

Glass Hollow Overlook; Side trail to Humpback Visitors Center

664

Distance from Springer Mountain (miles)

828 829 830 831 832 833 834 835 836 837 838 839 840 841 842 843 844 845 846 847 848 849 850 851

VIRGINIA

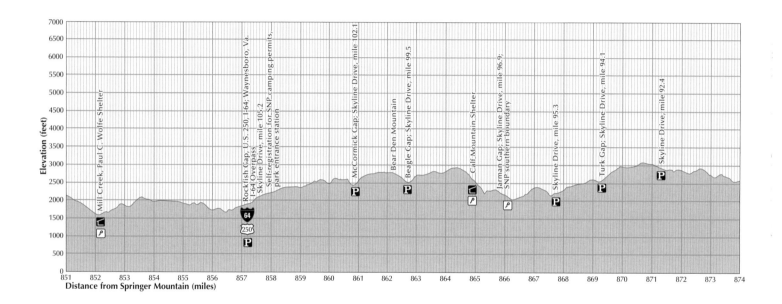

Elevation (feet)

Mill Creek, Paul C. Wolfe Shelter

Rockfish Gap, U.S. 250, I-64; Waynesboro, Va.
I-64 Overpass
Skyline Drive, mile 105.2
Self-registration for SNP camping permits,
park entrance station

McCormick Gap; Skyline Drive, mile 102.1

Bear Den Mountain
Beagle Gap; Skyline Drive, mile 99.5

Calf Mountain Shelter

Jarman Gap; Skyline Drive, mile 96.9;
SNP southern boundary

Skyline Drive, mile 95.3

Turk Gap; Skyline Drive, mile 94.1

Skyline Drive, mile 92.4

Distance from Springer Mountain (miles)

Appalachian Trail Guide to Shenandoah National Park →

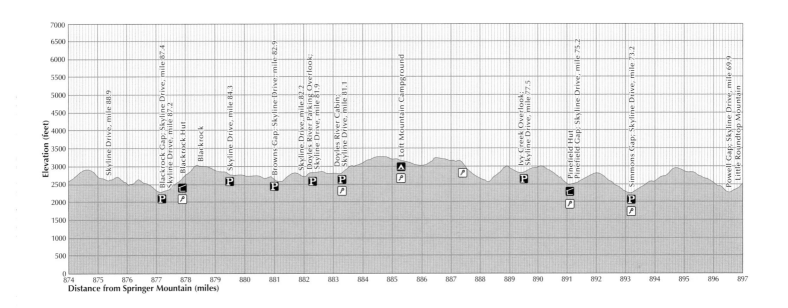

Elevation (feet)

7000
6500
6000
5500
5000
4500
4000
3500
3000
2500
2000
1500
1000
500
0

Skyline Drive, mile 88.9

Blackrock Gap; Skyline Drive, mile 87.4
Skyline Drive, mile 87.2
Blackrock Hut

Blackrock

Skyline Drive, mile 84.3

Browns Gap; Skyline Drive, mile 82.9

Skyline Drive, mile 82.2
Doyles River Parking Overlook;
Skyline Drive, mile 81.9

Doyles River Cabin;
Skyline Drive, mile 81.1

Loft Mountain Campground

Ivy Creek Overlook;
Skyline Drive, mile 77.5

Pinefield Hut
Pinefield Gap; Skyline Drive, mile 75.2

Simmons Gap; Skyline Drive, mile 73.2

Powell Gap; Skyline Drive, mile 69.9
Little Roundtop Mountain

Distance from Springer Mountain (miles)

874 875 876 877 878 879 880 881 882 883 884 885 886 887 888 889 890 891 892 893 894 895 896 897

VIRGINIA

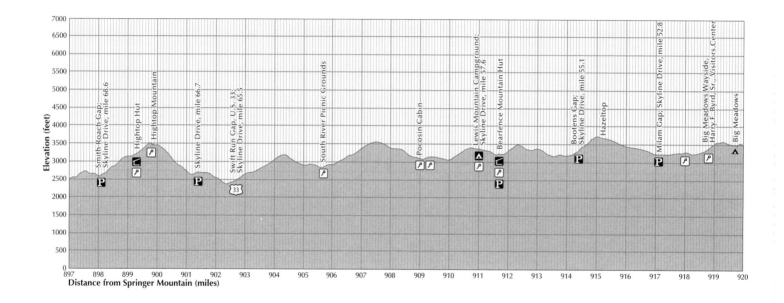

Elevation (feet)

Distance from Springer Mountain (miles)

Smith-Roach-Gap;
Skyline Drive, mile 68.6

Hightop Hut

Hightop Mountain

Skyline Drive, mile 66.7

Swift Run Gap, U.S. 33;
Skyline Drive, mile 65.5

South River Picnic Grounds

Pocosin Cabin

Lewis Mountain Campground;
Skyline Drive, mile 57.6

Bearfence Mountain Hut

Bootens Gap;
Skyline Drive, mile 55.1

Hazeltop

Milam Gap; Skyline Drive, mile 52.8

Big Meadows Wayside,
Harry F. Byrd, Sr., Visitors Center

Big Meadows

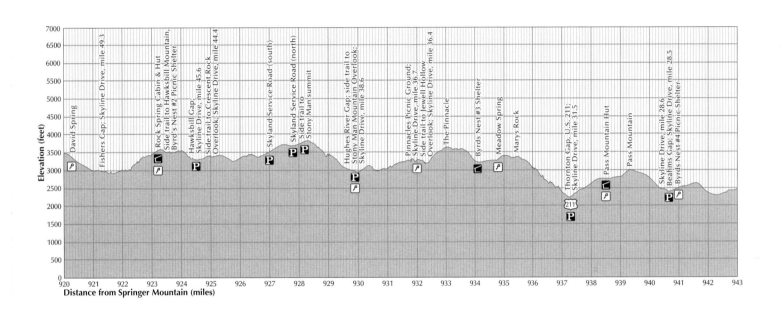

Elevation (feet)

David Spring

Fishers Gap; Skyline Drive, mile 49.3

Rock Spring Cabin & Hut
Side trail to Hawksbill Mountain,
Byrd's Nest #2 Picnic Shelter

Hawksbill Gap;
Skyline Drive, mile 45.6

Side trail to Crescent Rock
Overlook; Skyline Drive, mile 44.4

Skyland Service Road (south)

Skyland Service Road (north)
Side trail to
Stony Man summit

Hughes River Gap; side trail to
Stony Man Mountain Overlook;
Skyline Drive, mile 38.6

Pinnacles Picnic Ground;
Skyline Drive, mile 36.7
Side trail to Jewell Hollow
Overlook; Skyline Drive, mile 36.4

The Pinnacle

Byrds Nest #3 Shelter

Meadow Spring

Mary's Rock

Thornton Gap, U.S. 211;
Skyline Drive, mile 31.5

Pass Mountain Hut

Pass Mountain

Skyline Drive, mile 28.6
Beahms Gap; Skyline Drive, mile 28.5
Byrds Nest #4 Picnic Shelter

Distance from Springer Mountain (miles)

VIRGINIA

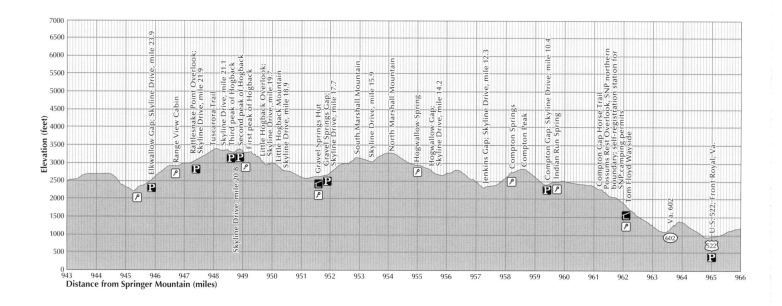

Elevation (feet)

7000
6500
6000
5500
5000
4500
4000
3500
3000
2500
2000
1500
1000
500
0

Elkwallow Gap; Skyline Drive, mile 23.9
Range View Cabin
Rattlesnake Point Overlook; Skyline Drive, mile 21.9
Tuscarora Trail
Skyline Drive, mile 21.1
Third peak of Hogback
Second peak of Hogback
First peak of Hogback
Skyline Drive, mile 20.8
Little Hogback Overlook; Skyline Drive, mile 19.7
Little Hogback Mountain
Skyline Drive, mile 18.9
Gravel Springs Hut
Gravel Springs Gap; Skyline Drive, mile 17.7
South Marshall Mountain
Skyline Drive, mile 15.9
North Marshall Mountain
Hogwallow Spring
Hogwallow Gap; Skyline Drive, mile 14.2
Jenkins Gap; Skyline Drive, mile 12.3
Compton Springs
Compton Peak
Compton Gap; Skyline Drive, mile 10.4
Indian Run Spring
Compton Gap Horse Trail
Possums Rest Overlook; SNP northern boundary; self-registration station for SNP camping permits
Tom Floyd Wayside
Va. 602
U.S. 522; Front-Royal, Va.

602
522

Distance from Springer Mountain (miles)

943 944 945 946 947 948 949 950 951 952 953 954 955 956 957 958 959 960 961 962 963 964 965 966

Elevation (feet)

7000
6500
6000
5500
5000
4500
4000
3500
3000
2500
2000
1500
1000
500
0

Mosby Campsite, Tom Sealock Spring
Jim & Molly Denton Shelter
Va. 638
Va. 55; Linden, Va.
Manassas Gap Shelter
Trillium Trail
Dick's Dome Shelter
Sky Meadows State Park Side Trail
Ashby Gap, U.S. 50
Rod Hollow Shelter

966 967 968 969 970 971 972 973 974 975 976 977 978 979 980 981 982 983 984 985 986 987 988 989

Distance from Springer Mountain (miles)

Appalachian Trail Guide to Maryland and Northern Virginia →

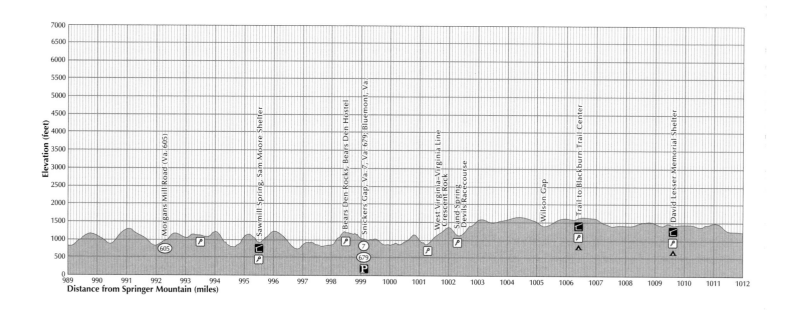

Appalachian Trail Book of Profiles

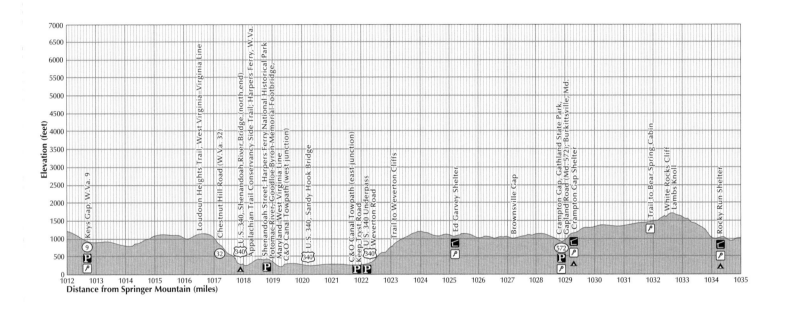

Elevation (feet) (vertical axis: 0, 500, 1000, 1500, 2000, 2500, 3000, 3500, 4000, 4500, 5000, 5500, 6000, 6500, 7000)

Distance from Springer Mountain (miles) (horizontal axis: 1012 to 1035)

Labels along the profile:
- Keys Gap, W.Va. 9
- Loudoun Heights Trail; West Virginia–Virginia Line
- Chestnut Hill Road (W.Va. 32)
- U.S. 340, Shenandoah River Bridge (north end)
- Appalachian Trail Conservancy Side Trail; Harpers Ferry, W.Va.
- Shenandoah Street; Harpers Ferry National Historical Park
- Potomac River; Goodloe-Byron-Memorial-Footbridge;
- Maryland–West Virginia Line
- C&O Canal Towpath (west junction)
- U.S. 340, Sandy Hook Bridge
- C&O Canal Towpath (east junction)
- Keep Tryst Road
- U.S. 340 Underpass
- Weverton Road
- Trail to Weverton Cliffs
- Ed Garvey Shelter
- Brownsville Gap
- Crampton Gap; Gathland State Park;
- Gapland Road (Md-572); Burkittsville, Md.
- Crampton Gap Shelter
- Trail to Bear Spring Cabin
- White Rocks Cliff
- Lambs Knoll
- Rocky Run Shelter

MARYLAND

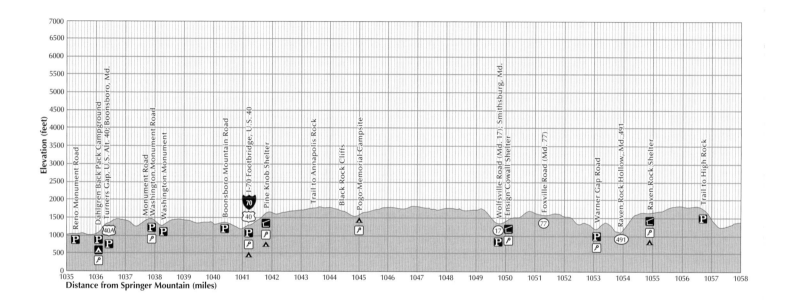

Elevation (feet)

Distance from Springer Mountain (miles)

Labels along profile (left to right):
Reno Monument Road
Dahlgren Back Pack Campground
Turners Gap, U.S. Alt. 40; Boonsboro, Md.
Monument Road
Washington Monument Road
Washington Monument
Boonsboro Mountain Road
I-70 Footbridge, U.S. 40
Pine Knob Shelter
Trail to Annapolis Rock
Black Rock Cliffs
Pogo Memorial Campsite
Wolfsville Road (Md. 17); Smithsburg, Md.
Ensign Cowall Shelter
Foxville Road (Md. 77)
Warner Gap Road
Raven Rock Hollow, Md. 491
Raven Rock Shelter
Trail to High Rock

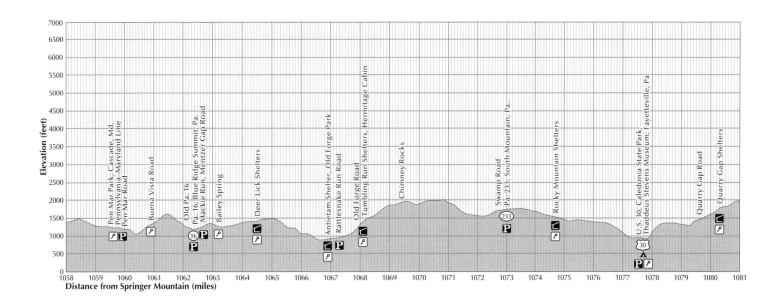

Elevation (feet)

7000
6500
6000
5500
5000
4500
4000
3500
3000
2500
2000
1500
1000
500
0

Distance from Springer Mountain (miles)

1058 1059 1060 1061 1062 1063 1064 1065 1066 1067 1068 1069 1070 1071 1072 1073 1074 1075 1076 1077 1078 1079 1080 1081

Pen Mar Park; Cascade, Md.
Pennsylvania–Maryland Line
Pen-Mar Road

Buena Vista Road

Old Pa. 16
Pa. 16; Blue Ridge Summit, Pa.
Mackie Run, Mentzer Gap Road

Bailey Spring

Deer Lick Shelters

Antietam Shelter, Old Forge Park
Rattlesnake Run Road

Old Forge Road
Tumbling Run Shelters, Hermitage Cabin

Chimney Rocks

Swamp Road
Pa. 233; South Mountain, Pa.

Rocky Mountain Shelters

U.S. 30; Caledonia State Park;
Thaddeus Stevens Museum; Fayetteville, Pa.

Quarry Gap Road

Quarry Gap Shelters

Appalachian Trail Guide to Pennsylvania →

PENNSYLVANIA

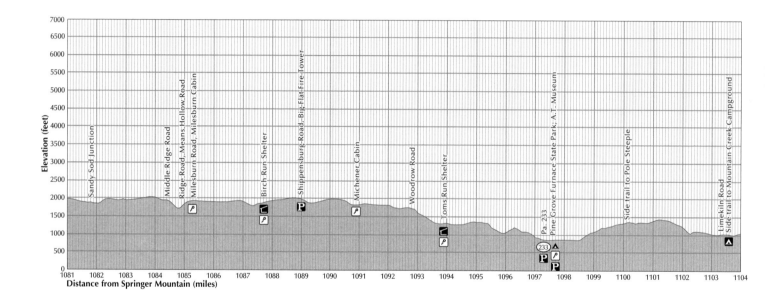

Elevation (feet)

Distance from Springer Mountain (miles)

Labels (left to right):
Sandy Sod Junction
Middle Ridge Road
Ridge Road; Means Hollow Road
Milesburn Road; Milesburn Cabin
Birch Run Shelter
Shippensburg Road; Big Flat Fire Tower
Michener Cabin
Woodrow Road
Toms Run Shelter
Pa. 233
Pine Grove Furnace State Park; A.T. Museum
Side trail to Pole Steeple
Limekiln Road
Side trail to Mountain Creek Campground

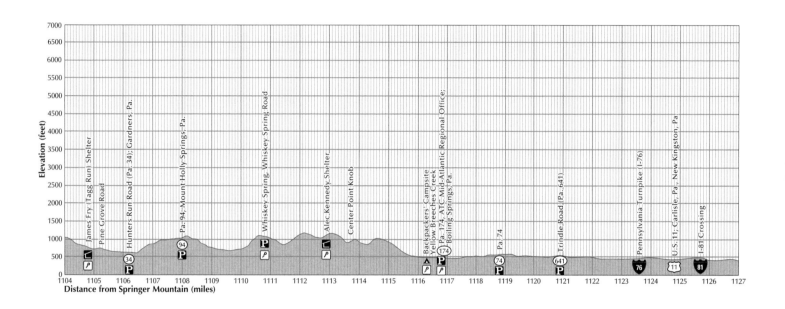

Elevation (feet)

7000
6500
6000
5500
5000
4500
4000
3500
3000
2500
2000
1500
1000
500
0

James Fry (Tagg Run) Shelter
Pine Grove Road
Hunters Run Road (Pa. 34); Gardners, Pa.
Pa. 94; Mount Holly Springs, Pa.
Whiskey Spring; Whiskey Spring Road
Alec Kennedy Shelter
Center Point Knob
Backpackers' Campsite
Yellow Breeches Creek
Pa. 174; ATC Mid-Atlantic Regional Office;
Boiling Springs, Pa.
Pa. 74
Trindle Road (Pa. 641)
Pennsylvania Turnpike (I-76)
U.S. 11; Carlisle, Pa.; New Kingston, Pa.
I-81 Crossing

94
34
74
174
641
76
11
81

Distance from Springer Mountain (miles)

1104 1105 1106 1107 1108 1109 1110 1111 1112 1113 1114 1115 1116 1117 1118 1119 1120 1121 1122 1123 1124 1125 1126 1127

PENNSYLVANIA

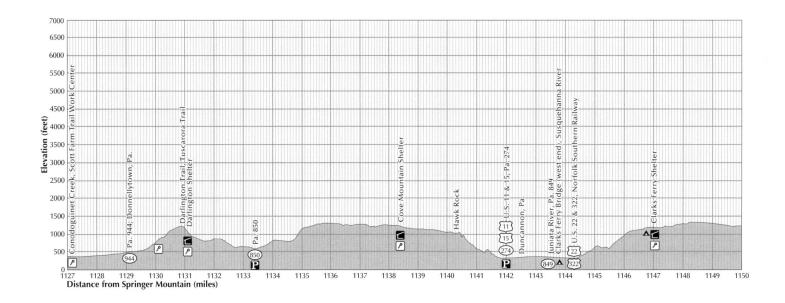

Elevation (feet)

7000
6500
6000
5500
5000
4500
4000
3500
3000
2500
2000
1500
1000
500
0

Conodoguinet Creek, Scott Farm Trail Work Center

Pa. 944; Donnellytown, Pa.

Darlington Trail, Tuscarora Trail
Darlington Shelter

Pa. 850

Cove Mountain Shelter

Hawk Rock

U.S. 11 & 15; Pa. 274
Duncannon, Pa.

Juniata River, Pa. 849
Clarks Ferry Bridge (west end), Susquehanna River

U.S. 22 & 322, Norfolk Southern Railway

Clarks Ferry Shelter

Distance from Springer Mountain (miles)

1127 1128 1129 1130 1131 1132 1133 1134 1135 1136 1137 1138 1139 1140 1141 1142 1143 1144 1145 1146 1147 1148 1149 1150

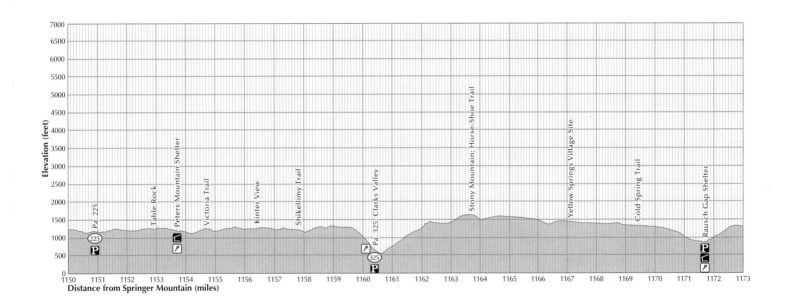

Elevation (feet)

7000
6500
6000
5500
5000
4500
4000
3500
3000
2500
2000
1500
1000
500
0

Pa. 225
Table Rock
Peters Mountain Shelter
Victoria Trail
Kinter View
Shikellimy Trail
Pa. 325, Clarks Valley
Stony Mountain; Horse-Shoe Trail
Yellow Springs Village Site
Cold Spring Trail
Rausch Gap Shelter

Distance from Springer Mountain (miles)

1150 1151 1152 1153 1154 1155 1156 1157 1158 1159 1160 1161 1162 1163 1164 1165 1166 1167 1168 1169 1170 1171 1172 1173

PENNSYLVANIA

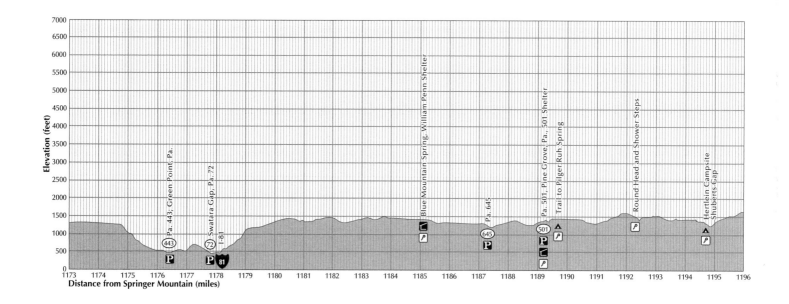

Elevation (feet)

Distance from Springer Mountain (miles)

Pa. 443; Green Point, Pa.

Swatara Gap, Pa. 72

I-81

Blue Mountain Spring, William Penn Shelter

Pa. 645

Pa. 501, Pine Grove, Pa., 501 Shelter

Trail to Pilger Ruh Spring

Round Head and Shower Steps

Hertlein Campsite
Shuberts Gap

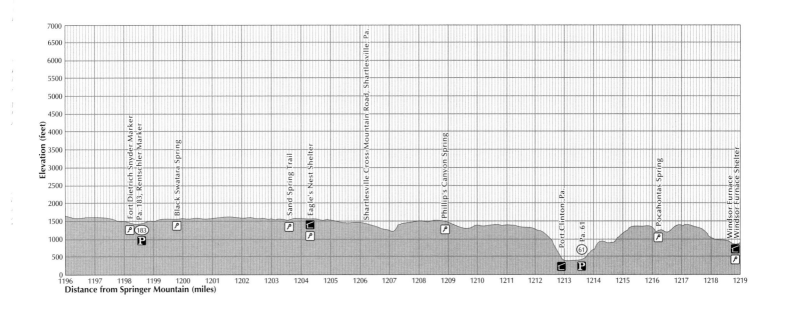

Elevation (feet)

Distance from Springer Mountain (miles)

Fort Dietrich Snyder Marker
Pa. 183, Rentschler Marker

Black Swatara Spring

Sand Spring Trail

Eagle's Nest Shelter

Shartlesville Cross-Mountain Road, Shartlesville, Pa.

Phillip's Canyon Spring

Port Clinton, Pa.

Pa. 61

Pocahontas Spring

Windsor Furnace
Windsor Furnace Shelter

Appalachian Trail Book of Profiles

PENNSYLVANIA

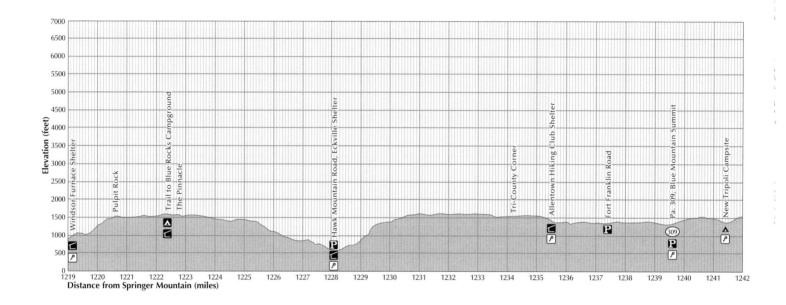

Elevation (feet)

Distance from Springer Mountain (miles)

Windsor Furnace Shelter
Pulpit Rock
Trail to Blue Rocks Campground
The Pinnacle
Hawk Mountain Road, Eckville Shelter
Tri-County Corner
Allentown Hiking Club Shelter
Fort Franklin Road
Pa. 309, Blue Mountain Summit
New Tripoli Campsite

Appalachian Trail Book of Profiles

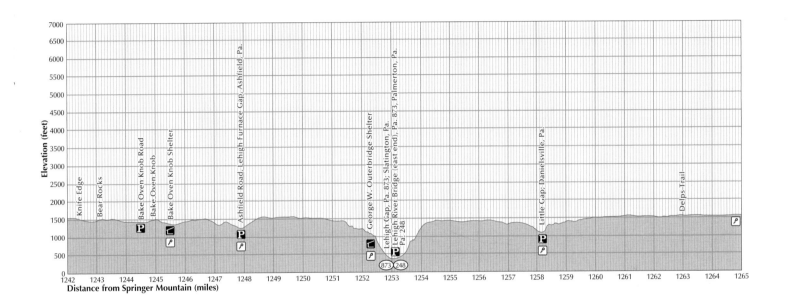

Elevation (feet)

7000
6500
6000
5500
5000
4500
4000
3500
3000
2500
2000
1500
1000
500
0

1242 1243 1244 1245 1246 1247 1248 1249 1250 1251 1252 1253 1254 1255 1256 1257 1258 1259 1260 1261 1262 1263 1264 1265

Distance from Springer Mountain (miles)

Knife Edge

Bear Rocks

Bake Oven Knob Road

Bake Oven Knob

Bake Oven Knob Shelter

Ashfield Road, Lehigh Furnace Gap, Ashfield, Pa.

George W. Outerbridge Shelter

Lehigh Gap, Pa. 873; Slatington, Pa.

Lehigh River Bridge (east end), Pa. 873, Palmerton, Pa.

Pa. 248

Little Gap; Danielsville, Pa.

Delps Trail

873 248

Appalachian Trail Book of Profiles

55

PENNSYLVANIA

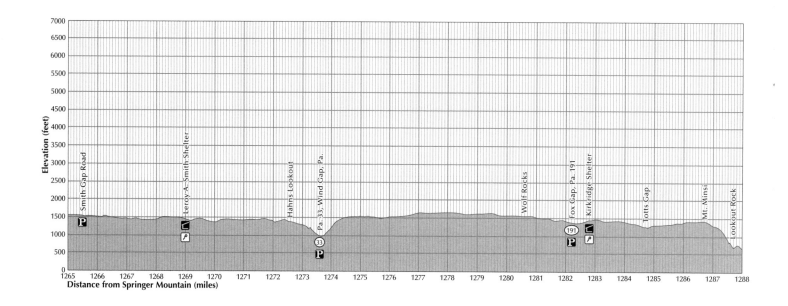

Elevation (feet)

Distance from Springer Mountain (miles)

Smith Gap Road

Leroy A. Smith Shelter

Hahns Lookout

Pa. 33, Wind Gap, Pa.

Wolf Rocks

Fox Gap, Pa. 191

Kirkridge Shelter

Totts Gap

Mt. Minsi

Lookout Rock

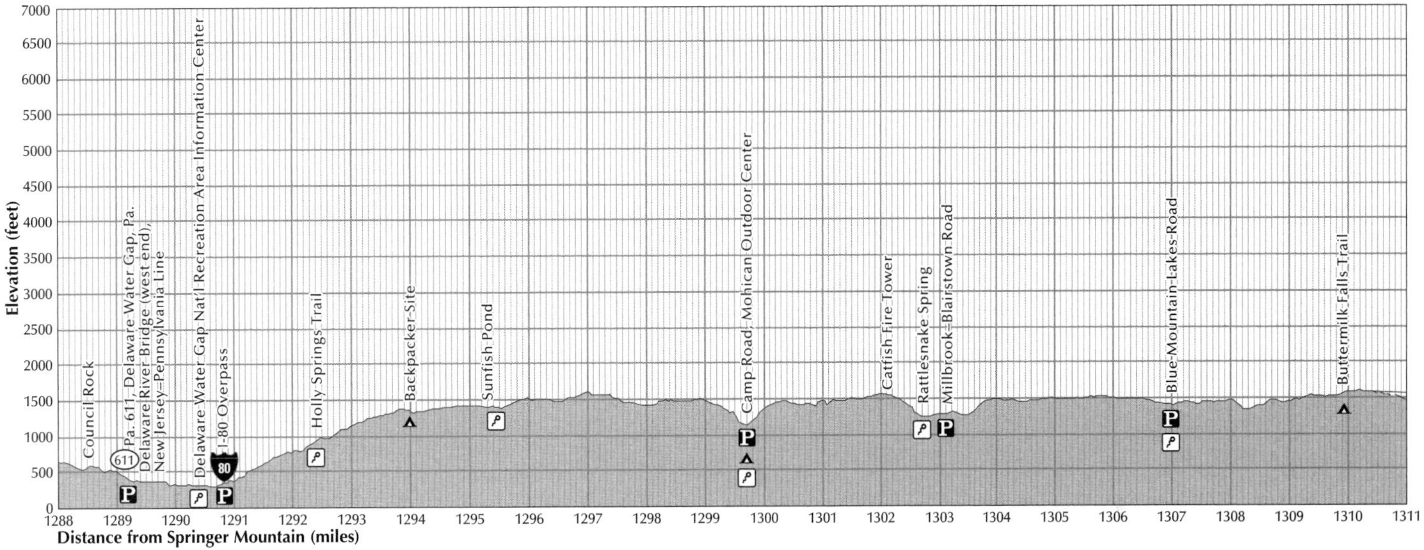
Elevation (feet)
7000
6500
6000
5500
5000
4500
4000
3500
3000
2500
2000
1500
1000
500
0
Council Rock
611
Pa. 611, Delaware Water Gap, Pa.
Delaware River Bridge (west end),
New Jersey–Pennsylvania Line
Delaware Water Gap Nat'l Recreation Area Information Center
80
I-80 Overpass
Holly Springs Trail
Backpacker Site
Sunfish Pond
Camp Road, Mohican Outdoor Center
Catfish Fire Tower
Rattlesnake Spring
Millbrook–Blairstown Road
Blue Mountain Lakes Road
Buttermilk Falls Trail
1288
1289
1290
1291
1292
1293
1294
1295
1296
1297
1298
1299
1300
1301
1302
1303
1304
1305
1306
1307
1308
1309
1310
1311
Distance from Springer Mountain (miles)

Appalachian Trail Guide to New York–New Jersey →

NEW JERSEY

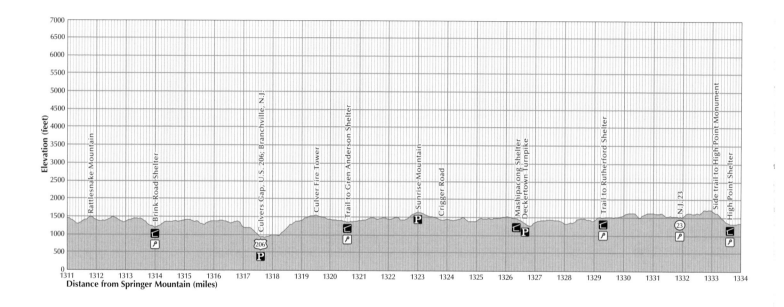

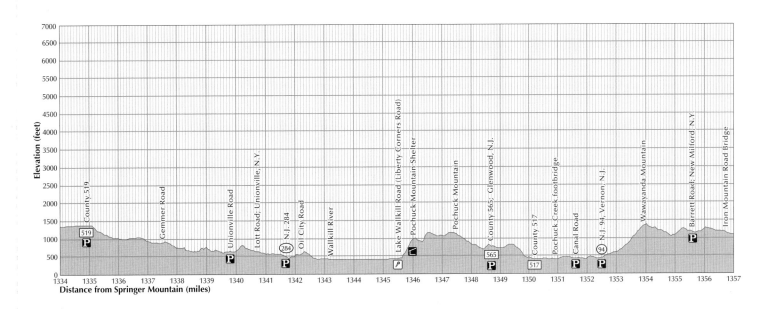

Elevation (feet)

7000
6500
6000
5500
5000
4500
4000
3500
3000
2500
2000
1500
1000
500
0

County 519

519
P

Gemmer Road

Unionville Road

P

Lott Road; Unionville, N.Y.

N.J. 284

284

Oil City Road

P

Wallkill River

Lake Wallkill Road (Liberty Corners Road)

Pochuck Mountain Shelter

Pochuck Mountain

County 565; Glenwood, N.J.

565

P

County 517

517

Pochuck Creek footbridge

Canal Road

P

N.J. 94; Vernon, N.J.

94

P

Wawayanda Mountain

Barrett Road; New Milford, N.Y.

P

Iron Mountain Road Bridge

Distance from Springer Mountain (miles)

1334 1335 1336 1337 1338 1339 1340 1341 1342 1343 1344 1345 1346 1347 1348 1349 1350 1351 1352 1353 1354 1355 1356 1357

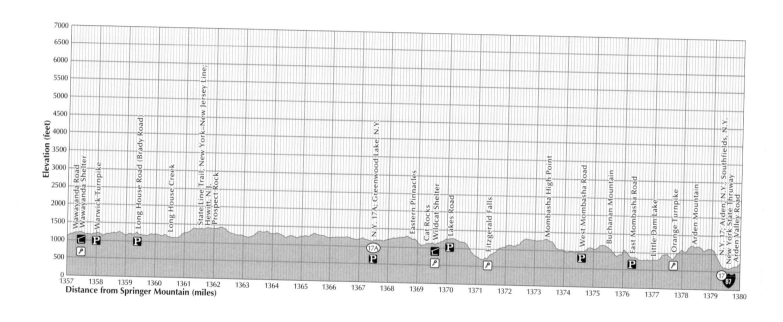

Elevation (feet)

Distance from Springer Mountain (miles)

Wawayanda Road
Wawayanda Shelter
Warwick Turnpike
Long House Road (Brady Road)
Long House Creek
State Line Trail; New York–New Jersey Line; Hewitt, N.J.
Prospect Rock
N.Y. 17A; Greenwood Lake, N.Y.
Eastern Pinnacles
Cat Rocks
Wildcat Shelter
Lakes Road
Fitzgerald Falls
Mombasha High Point
West Mombasha Road
Buchanan Mountain
East Mombasha Road
Little Dam Lake
Orange Turnpike
Arden Mountain
N.Y. 17; Arden, N.Y.; Southfields, N.Y.
New York State Thruway
Arden Valley Road

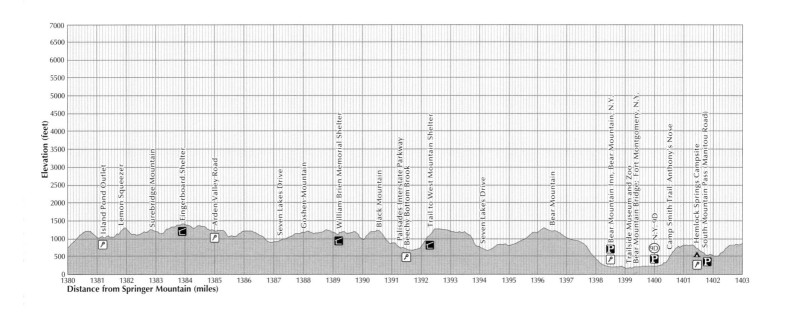

Island Pond Outlet
Lemon Squeezer
Surebridge Mountain
Fingerboard Shelter
Arden Valley Road
Seven Lakes Drive
Goshen Mountain
William Brien Memorial Shelter
Black Mountain
Palisades Interstate Parkway
Beechy Bottom Brook
Trail to West Mountain Shelter
Seven Lakes Drive
Bear Mountain
Bear Mountain Inn, Bear Mountain, N.Y.
Trailside Museum and Zoo
Bear Mountain Bridge; Fort Montgomery, N.Y.
N.Y.-9D
Camp Smith Trail; Anthony's Nose
Hemlock Springs Campsite
South Mountain Pass (Manitou Road)

Elevation (feet)

7000
6500
6000
5500
5000
4500
4000
3500
3000
2500
2000
1500
1000
500
0

1380 1381 1382 1383 1384 1385 1386 1387 1388 1389 1390 1391 1392 1393 1394 1395 1396 1397 1398 1399 1400 1401 1402 1403

Distance from Springer Mountain (miles)

NEW YORK

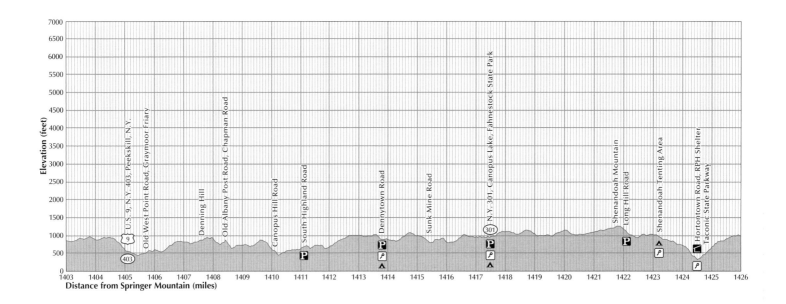

Elevation (feet)

Distance from Springer Mountain (miles)

Labels on profile (left to right):
U.S. 9, N.Y. 403, Peekskill, N.Y.
Old West Point Road, Graymoor Friary
Denning Hill
Old Albany Post Road, Chapman Road
Canopus Hill Road
South Highland Road
Dennytown Road
Sunk Mine Road
N.Y. 301, Canopus Lake, Fahnestock State Park
Shenandoah Mountain
Long Hill Road
Shenandoah Tenting Area
Hortontown Road, RPH Shelter
Taconic State Parkway

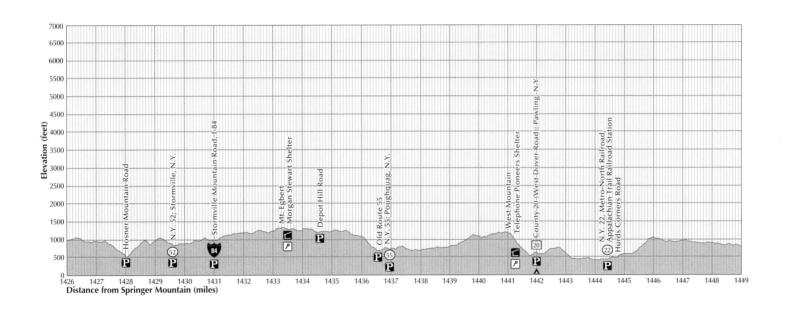

Elevation (feet)

7000
6500
6000
5500
5000
4500
4000
3500
3000
2500
2000
1500
1000
500
0

Hosner Mountain Road
N.Y. 52; Stormville, N.Y. ⓢ52
Stormville-Mountain-Road;-I-84 84
Mt. Egbert
Morgan Stewart Shelter
Depot Hill Road
Old Route 55
N.Y. 55; Poughquag, N.Y. ⓢ55
West Mountain
Telephone Pioneers Shelter
County 20 (West-Dover-Road); Pawling, N.Y. 20
N.Y. 22; Metro-North Railroad;
Appalachian Trail Railroad Station ⓢ22
Hurds Corners Road

Distance from Springer Mountain (miles)

1426 1427 1428 1429 1430 1431 1432 1433 1434 1435 1436 1437 1438 1439 1440 1441 1442 1443 1444 1445 1446 1447 1448 1449

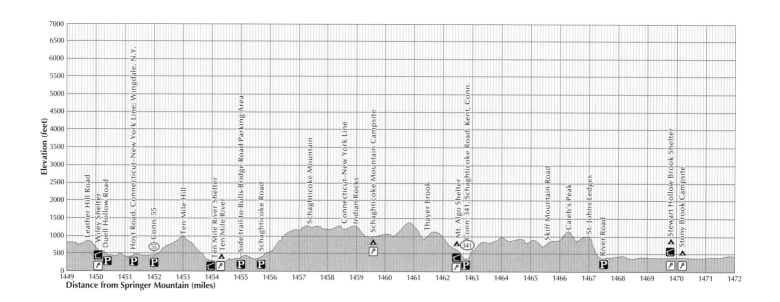

Elevation (feet)

- Leather Hill Road
- Wiley Shelter
- Duell Hollow Road
- Hoyt Road, Connecticut–New York Line; Wingdale, N.Y.
- Conn. 55
- Ten-Mile-Hill
- Ten Mile River Shelter
- Ten Mile River
- Side trail to Bulls-Bridge-Road-Parking-Area
- Schaghticoke Road
- Schaghticoke Mountain
- Connecticut–New York Line
- Indian-Rocks
- Schaghticoke Mountain Campsite
- Thayer Brook
- Mt. Algo Shelter
- Conn. 341, Schaghticoke Road, Kent, Conn.
- Skiff Mountain Road
- Caleb's Peak
- St.-Johns-Ledges
- River Road
- Stewart Hollow Brook Shelter
- Stony Brook Campsite

Distance from Springer Mountain (miles)

Appalachian Trail Guide to Massachusetts–Connecticut →

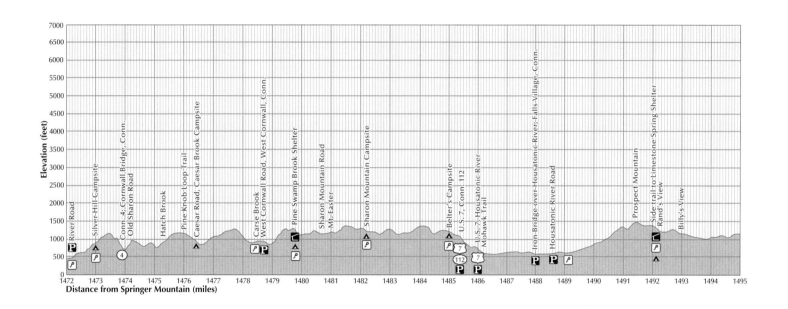

Elevation (feet)

7000
6500
6000
5500
5000
4500
4000
3500
3000
2500
2000
1500
1000
500
0

River Road
Silver Hill Campsite
Conn. 4, Cornwall Bridge, Conn.
Old Sharon Road
Hatch Brook
Pine Knob Loop Trail
Caesar Road, Caesar Brook Campsite
Carse Brook
West Cornwall Road, West Cornwall, Conn.
Pine Swamp Brook Shelter
Sharon Mountain Road
Mt. Easter
Sharon Mountain Campsite
Belter's Campsite
U.S. 7, Conn. 112
U.S. 7, Housatonic River
Mohawk Trail
Iron Bridge over Housatonic River, Falls Village, Conn.
Housatonic River Road
Prospect Mountain
Side trail to Limestone Spring Shelter
Rand's View
Billy's View

Distance from Springer Mountain (miles)

1472 1473 1474 1475 1476 1477 1478 1479 1480 1481 1482 1483 1484 1485 1486 1487 1488 1489 1490 1491 1492 1493 1494 1495

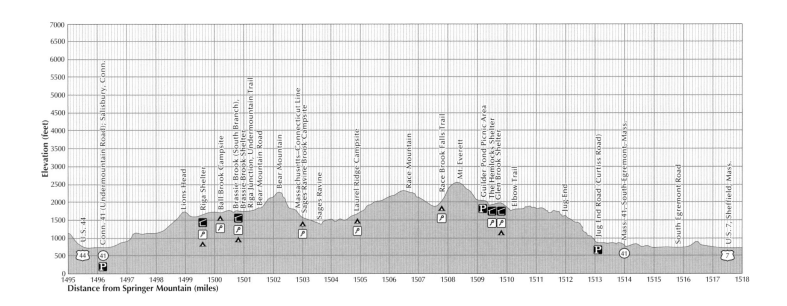

Elevation (feet)

Distance from Springer Mountain (miles)

U.S. 44

Conn. 41 (Undermountain Road); Salisbury, Conn.

Lions Head

Riga Shelter

Ball Brook Campsite

Brassie Brook (South Branch); Brassie Brook Shelter

Riga Junction, Undermountain Trail

Bear Mountain Road

Bear Mountain

Massachusetts–Connecticut Line
Sages Ravine Brook Campsite

Sage's Ravine

Laurel Ridge Campsite

Race Mountain

Race Brook Falls Trail

Mt. Everett

Guilder Pond Picnic Area
The Hemlocks Shelter
Glen Brook Shelter

Elbow Trail

Jug-End

Jug End Road (Curtiss Road)

Mass. 41–South-Egremont, Mass.

South Egremont Road

U.S. 7; Sheffield, Mass.

Appalachian Trail Book of Profiles

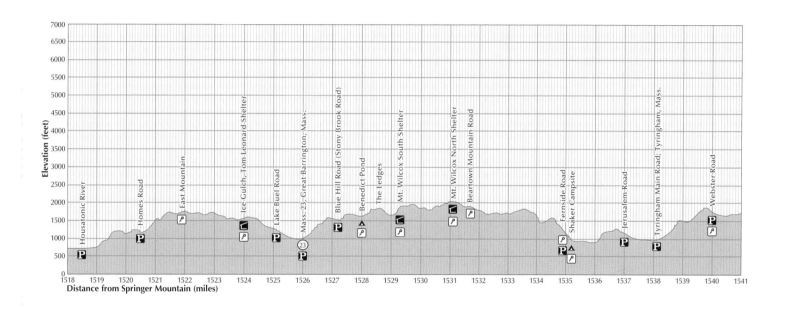

Elevation (feet)

7000
6500
6000
5500
5000
4500
4000
3500
3000
2500
2000
1500
1000
500
0

Housatonic River
Homes Road
East Mountain
Ice Gulch—Tom Leonard Shelter
Lake Buel Road
Mass. 23; Great Barrington, Mass.
Blue Hill Road (Stony Brook Road)
Benedict Pond
The Ledges
Mt. Wilcox South Shelter
Mt. Wilcox North Shelter
Beartown Mountain Road
Fernside Road
Shaker Campsite
Jerusalem Road
Tyringham Main Road; Tyringham, Mass.
Webster Road

Distance from Springer Mountain (miles)

1518 1519 1520 1521 1522 1523 1524 1525 1526 1527 1528 1529 1530 1531 1532 1533 1534 1535 1536 1537 1538 1539 1540 1541

MASSACHUSETTS

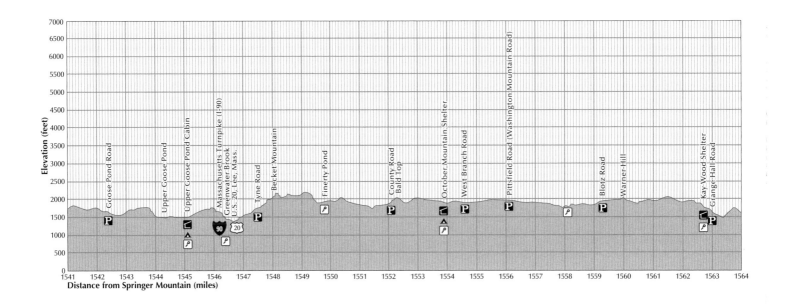

Elevation (feet)

Distance from Springer Mountain (miles)

Goose Pond Road
Upper Goose Pond
Upper Goose Pond Cabin
Massachusetts Turnpike (I-90)
Greenwater Brook
U.S. 20, Lee, Mass.
Tyne Road
Becket Mountain
Finerty Pond
County Road
Bald Top
October Mountain Shelter
West Branch Road
Pittsfield Road (Washington Mountain Road)
Blotz Road
Warner Hill
Kay Wood Shelter
Grange Hall Road

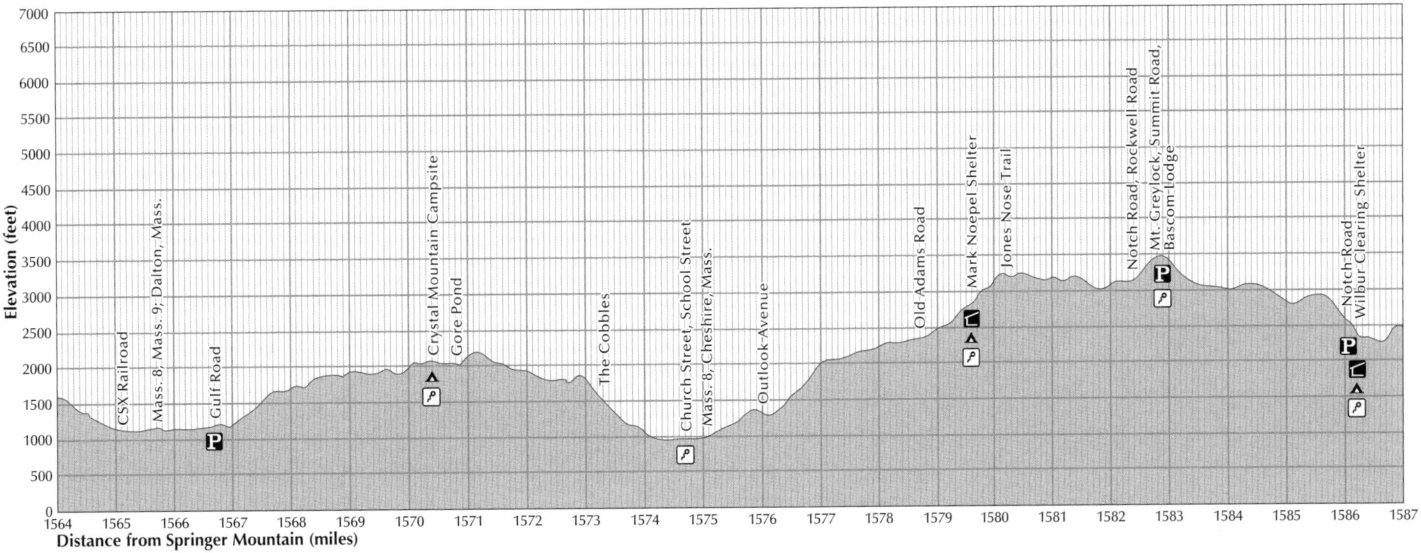

Elevation (feet)
7000
6500
6000
5500
5000
4500
4000
3500
3000
2500
2000
1500
1000
500
0
CSX Railroad
Mass. 8, Mass. 9; Dalton, Mass.
Gulf Road
Crystal Mountain Campsite
Gore Pond
The Cobbles
Church Street, School Street
Mass. 8; Cheshire, Mass.
Outlook Avenue
Old Adams Road
Mark Noepel Shelter
Jones Nose Trail
Notch Road, Rockwell Road
Mt. Greylock, Summit Road, Bascom Lodge
Notch Road
Wilbur Clearing Shelter
1564
1565
1566
1567
1568
1569
1570
1571
1572
1573
1574
1575
1576
1577
1578
1579
1580
1581
1582
1583
1584
1585
1586
1587
Distance from Springer Mountain (miles)

MASSACHUSETTS | VERMONT

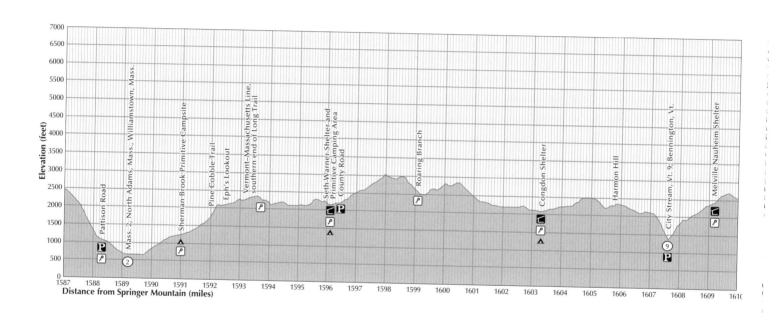

Elevation (feet)

7000
6500
6000
5500
5000
4500
4000
3500
3000
2500
2000
1500
1000
500
0

Pattison Road

Mass. 2, North Adams, Mass., Williamstown, Mass.

Sherman-Brook Primitive Campsite

Pine Cobble Trail

Eph's Lookout

Vermont–Massachusetts Line, southern end of Long Trail

Seth Warner Shelter and Primitive Camping Area

County Road

Roaring Branch

Congdon Shelter

Harmon Hill

City Stream, Vt. 9, Bennington, Vt.

Melville Nauheim Shelter

Distance from Springer Mountain (miles)

1587 1588 1589 1590 1591 1592 1593 1594 1595 1596 1597 1598 1599 1600 1601 1602 1603 1604 1605 1606 1607 1608 1609 1610

Appalachian Trail Guide to New Hampshire–Vermont →

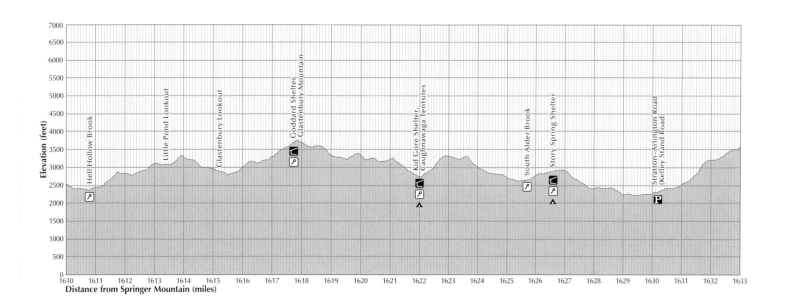

Elevation (feet)

7000
6500
6000
5500
5000
4500
4000
3500
3000
2500
2000
1500
1000
500
0

1610 1611 1612 1613 1614 1615 1616 1617 1618 1619 1620 1621 1622 1623 1624 1625 1626 1627 1628 1629 1630 1631 1632 1633

Distance from Springer Mountain (miles)

Hell Hollow Brook

Little Pond Lookout

Glastenbury Lookout

Goddard Shelter, Glastenbury Mountain

Kid Gore Shelter, Caughnawaga Tentsites

South Alder Brook

Story Spring Shelter

Stratton–Arlington Road (Kelley Stand Road)

VERMONT

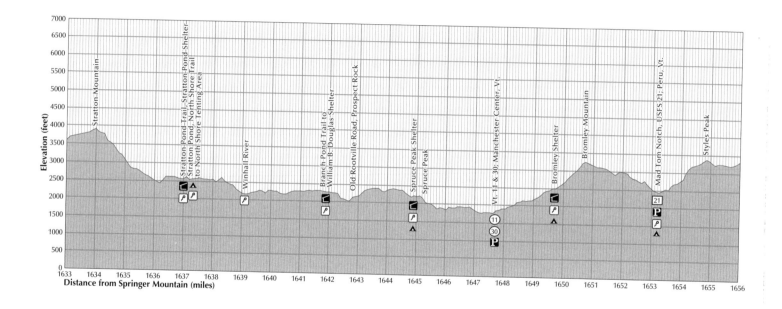

Elevation (feet)

Distance from Springer Mountain (miles)

Stratton Mountain

Stratton-Pond-Trail; Stratton-Pond-Shelter
Stratton Pond; North Shore Trail
to North Shore Tenting Area

Winhall River

Branch Pond Trail to
William-B.-Douglas-Shelter

Old Rootville Road; Prospect Rock

Spruce Peak Shelter
Spruce Peak

Vt. 11 & 30; Manchester Center, Vt.

Bromley Shelter

Bromley Mountain

Mad Tom Notch, USFS 21; Peru, Vt.

Styles Peak

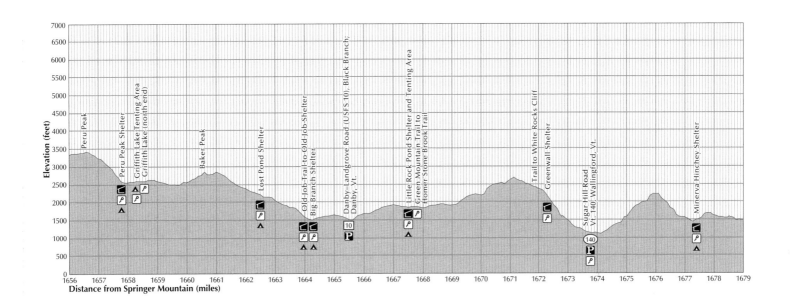

Elevation (feet)

7000
6500
6000
5500
5000
4500
4000
3500
3000
2500
2000
1500
1000
500
0

Peru Peak

Peru Peak Shelter

Griffith Lake Tenting Area
Griffith Lake (north end)

Baker Peak

Lost Pond Shelter

Old-Job-Trail-to-Old-Job-Shelter
Big Branch Shelter

Danby–Landgrove Road (USFS 10), Black Branch;
Danby, Vt.

Little Rock Pond Shelter and Tenting Area
Green Mountain Trail to
Homer Stone Brook Trail

Trail to White Rocks Cliff

Greenwall Shelter

Sugar Hill Road
Vt. 140; Wallingford, Vt.

Minerva Hinchey Shelter

Distance from Springer Mountain (miles)

1656 1657 1658 1659 1660 1661 1662 1663 1664 1665 1666 1667 1668 1669 1670 1671 1672 1673 1674 1675 1676 1677 1678 1679

VERMONT

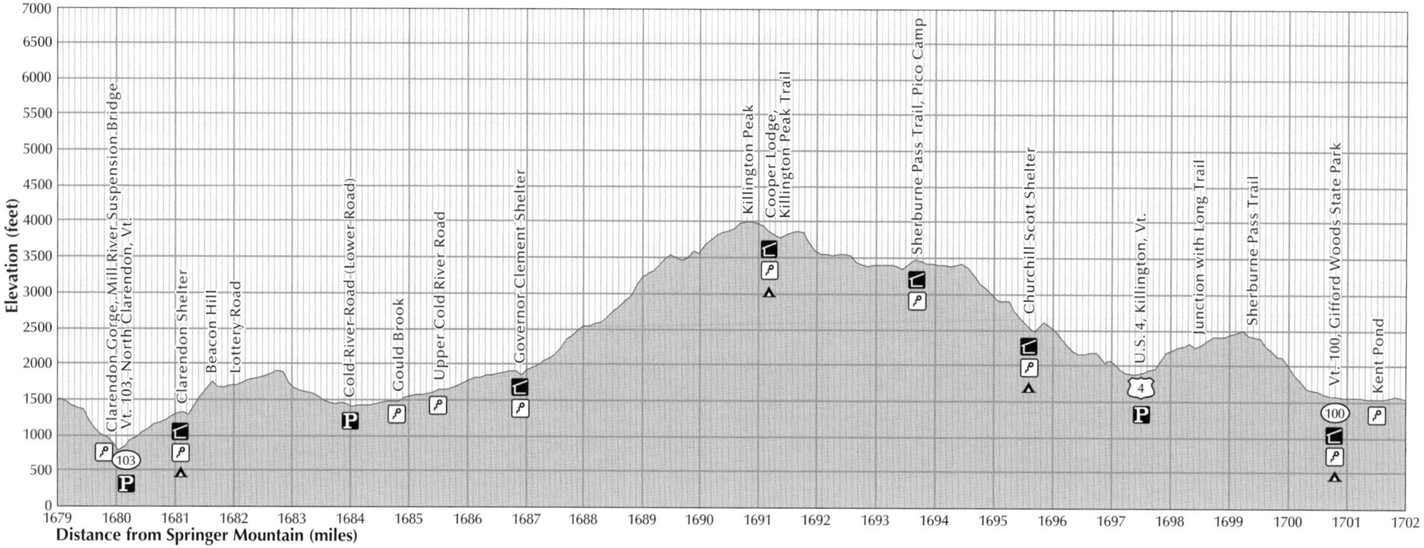

Elevation (feet)
7000
6500
6000
5500
5000
4500
4000
3500
3000
2500
2000
1500
1000
500
0
Clarendon Gorge, Mill River Suspension Bridge
Vt. 103, North Clarendon, Vt.
103
Clarendon Shelter
Beacon Hill
Lottery Road
Cold River Road (Lower Road)
Gould Brook
Upper Cold River Road
Governor Clement Shelter
Killington Peak
Cooper Lodge,
Killington Peak Trail
Sherburne Pass Trail, Pico Camp
Churchill Scott Shelter
U.S. 4, Killington, Vt.
4
Junction with Long Trail
Sherburne Pass Trail
Vt. 100, Gifford Woods State Park
100
Kent Pond
1679
1680
1681
1682
1683
1684
1685
1686
1687
1688
1689
1690
1691
1692
1693
1694
1695
1696
1697
1698
1699
1700
1701
1702
Distance from Springer Mountain (miles)

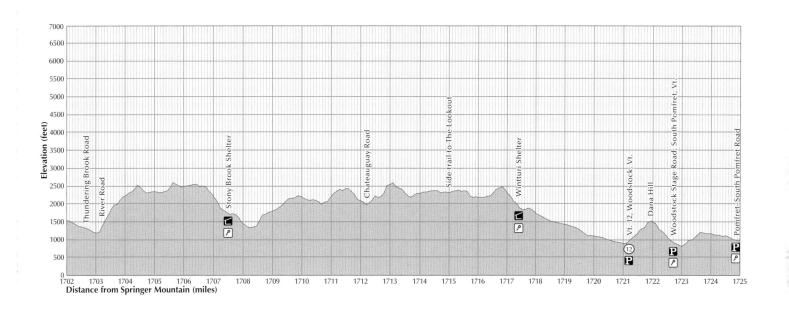

Elevation (feet)

7000
6500
6000
5500
5000
4500
4000
3500
3000
2500
2000
1500
1000
500
0

Thundering Brook Road
River Road
Stony Brook Shelter
Chateauguay Road
Side-trail-to-The-Lookout
Wintturi Shelter
Vt. 12, Woodstock, Vt.
Dana Hill
Woodstock Stage Road; South Pomfret, Vt.
Pomfret–South Pomfret Road

1702 1703 1704 1705 1706 1707 1708 1709 1710 1711 1712 1713 1714 1715 1716 1717 1718 1719 1720 1721 1722 1723 1724 1725

Distance from Springer Mountain (miles)

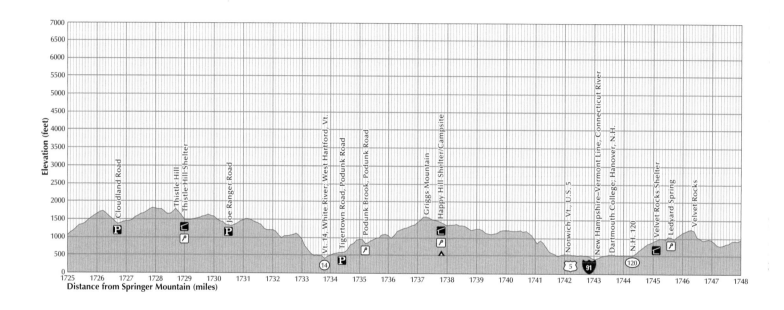

Elevation (feet)

Distance from Springer Mountain (miles)

Cloudland Road

Thistle Hill
Thistle Hill Shelter

Joe Ranger Road

Vt. 14, White River, West Hartford, Vt.
Tigertown Road, Podunk Road

Podunk Brook, Podunk Road

Griggs Mountain
Happy Hill Shelter/Campsite

Norwich, Vt., U.S. 5

New Hampshire–Vermont Line, Connecticut River
Dartmouth College; Hanover, N.H.

N.H. 120

Velvet Rocks Shelter
Ledyard Spring

Velvet Rocks

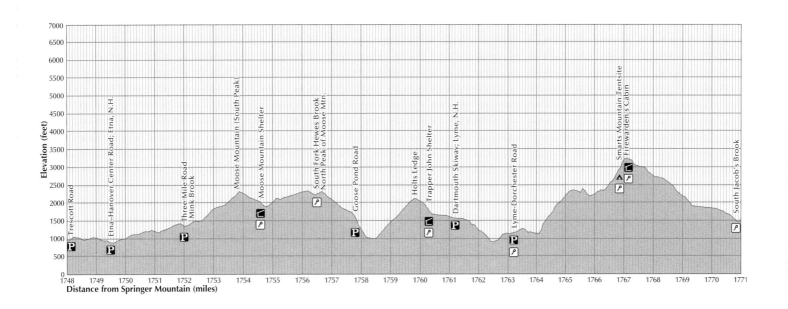

Elevation (feet)

7000
6500
6000
5500
5000
4500
4000
3500
3000
2500
2000
1500
1000
500
0

Trescott Road

Etna–Hanover Center Road; Etna, N.H.

Three-Mile-Road
Mink Brook

Moose Mountain (South Peak)

Moose Mountain Shelter

South Fork Hewes Brook
North Peak of Moose Mtn.

Goose Pond Road

Holts Ledge

Trapper John Shelter

Dartmouth Skiway; Lyme, N.H.

Lyme–Dorchester Road

Smarts Mountain Tentsite
Firewarden's Cabin

South Jacob's Brook

Distance from Springer Mountain (miles)

1748 1749 1750 1751 1752 1753 1754 1755 1756 1757 1758 1759 1760 1761 1762 1763 1764 1765 1766 1767 1768 1769 1770 1771

NEW HAMPSHIRE

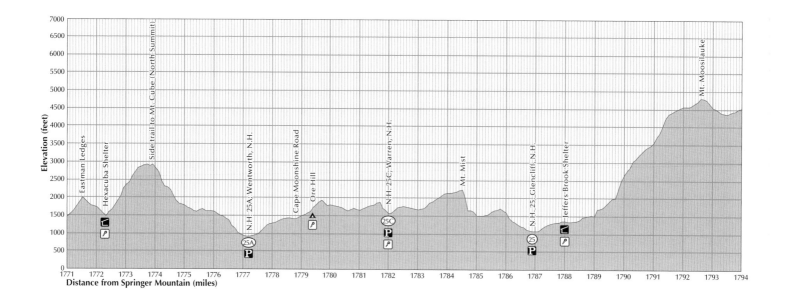

Elevation (feet)

Distance from Springer Mountain (miles)

Eastman Ledges
Hexacuba Shelter
Side trail to Mt. Cube (North Summit)
N.H. 25A; Wentworth, N.H.
Cape Moonshine Road
Ore Hill
N.H. 25C; Warren, N.H.
Mt. Mist
N.H. 25; Glencliff, N.H.
Jeffers Brook Shelter
Mt. Moosilauke

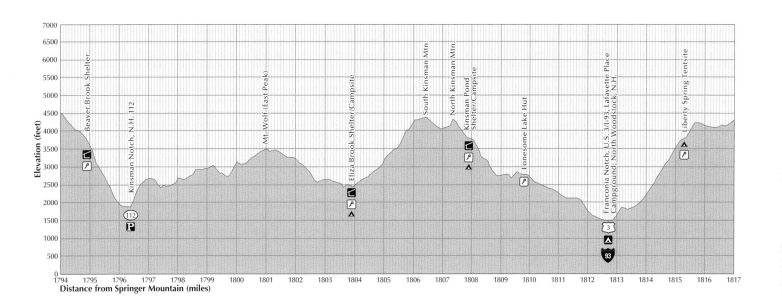

Elevation (feet)

7000
6500
6000
5500
5000
4500
4000
3500
3000
2500
2000
1500
1000
500
0

Beaver Brook Shelter

Kinsman Notch, N.H.; 112

112

P

Mt. Wolf (East Peak)

Eliza Brook Shelter/Campsite

South Kinsman Mtn.

North Kinsman Mtn.

Kinsman Pond Shelter/Campsite

Lonesome Lake Hut

Franconia Notch, U.S. 3/I-93; Lafayette Place Campground; North Woodstock, N.H.

3

93

Liberty Spring Tentsite

1794 1795 1796 1797 1798 1799 1800 1801 1802 1803 1804 1805 1806 1807 1808 1809 1810 1811 1812 1813 1814 1815 1816 1817

Distance from Springer Mountain (miles)

NEW HAMPSHIRE

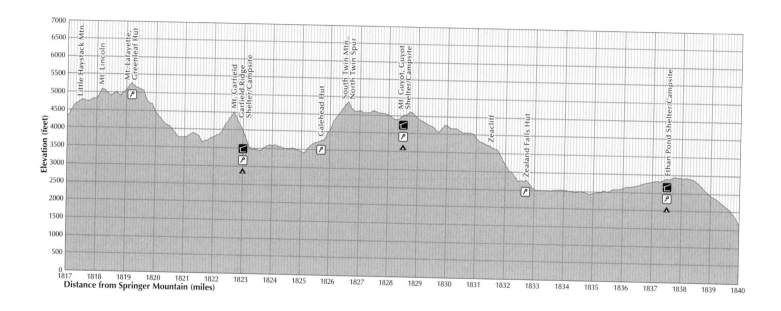

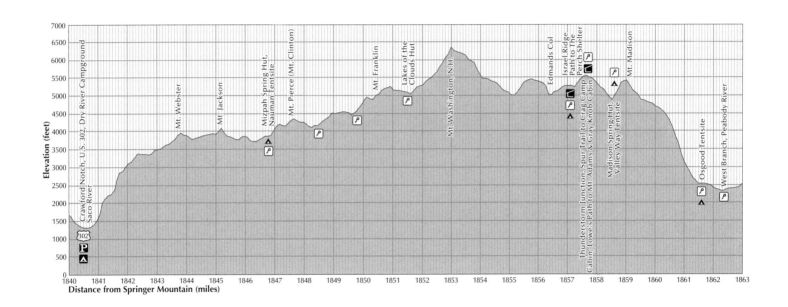

Elevation (feet)

7000
6500
6000
5500
5000
4500
4000
3500
3000
2500
2000
1500
1000
500
0

1840 1841 1842 1843 1844 1845 1846 1847 1848 1849 1850 1851 1852 1853 1854 1855 1856 1857 1858 1859 1860 1861 1862 1863

Distance from Springer Mountain (miles)

Crawford Notch, U.S. 302, Dry River Campground
Saco River

302

Mt. Webster

Mt. Jackson

Mizpah Spring Hut, Nauman Tentsite

Mt. Pierce (Mt. Clinton)

Mt. Franklin

Lakes of the Clouds Hut

Mt. Washington, N.H.

Edmands Col

Israel Ridge Path to The Perch Shelter

Thunderstorm Junction, Spur Trail to Crag Camp Cabin, Lowe's Path to Mt. Adams & Gray Knob Cabin

Madison Spring Hut, Valley Way Tentsite

Mt. Madison

Osgood Tentsite

West Branch, Peabody River

NEW HAMPSHIRE

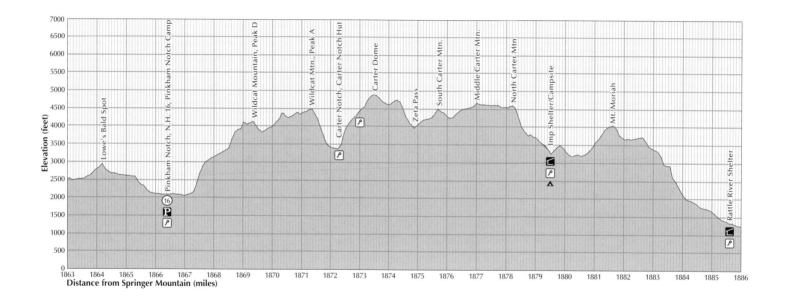

Elevation (feet) — vertical axis: 7000, 6500, 6000, 5500, 5000, 4500, 4000, 3500, 3000, 2500, 2000, 1500, 1000, 500, 0

Distance from Springer Mountain (miles): 1863, 1864, 1865, 1866, 1867, 1868, 1869, 1870, 1871, 1872, 1873, 1874, 1875, 1876, 1877, 1878, 1879, 1880, 1881, 1882, 1883, 1884, 1885, 1886

Labels on profile:
Lowe's Bald Spot
Pinkham Notch, N.H. 16, Pinkham Notch Camp
Wildcat Mountain, Peak D
Wildcat Mtn., Peak A
Carter Notch, Carter Notch Hut
Carter Dome
Zeta Pass
South Carter Mtn.
Middle Carter Mtn.
North Carter Mtn.
Imp Shelter/Campsite
Mt. Moriah
Rattle River Shelter

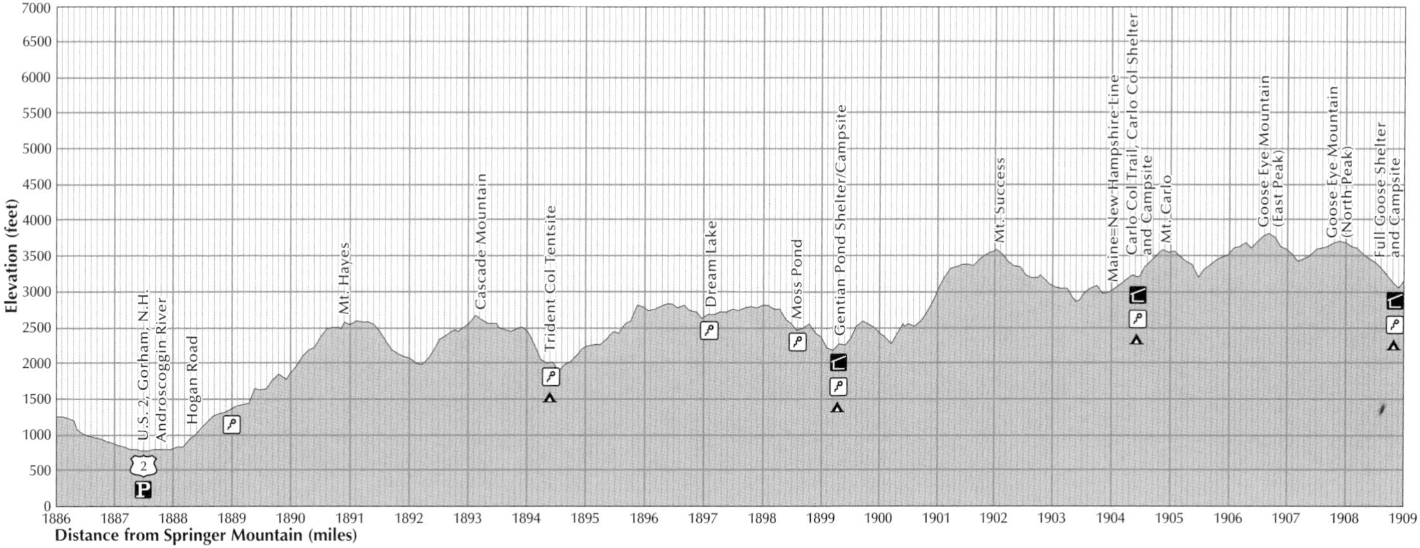
Elevation (feet)
7000
6500
6000
5500
5000
4500
4000
3500
3000
2500
2000
1500
1000
500
0
U.S. 2, Gorham, N.H.
Androscoggin River
Hogan Road
Mt. Hayes
Cascade Mountain
Trident Col Tentsite
Dream Lake
Moss Pond
Gentian Pond Shelter/Campsite
Mt. Success
Maine–New Hampshire Line
Carlo Col Trail, Carlo Col Shelter and Campsite
Mt. Carlo
Goose Eye Mountain (East Peak)
Goose Eye Mountain (North Peak)
Full Goose Shelter and Campsite
1886
1887
1888
1889
1890
1891
1892
1893
1894
1895
1896
1897
1898
1899
1900
1901
1902
1903
1904
1905
1906
1907
1908
1909
Distance from Springer Mountain (miles)

MAINE

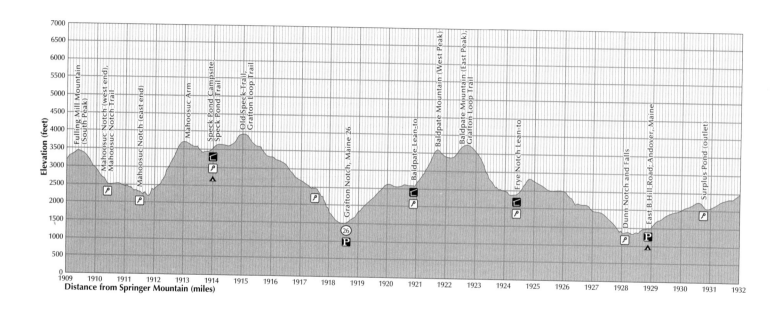

Appalachian Trail Guide to Maine →

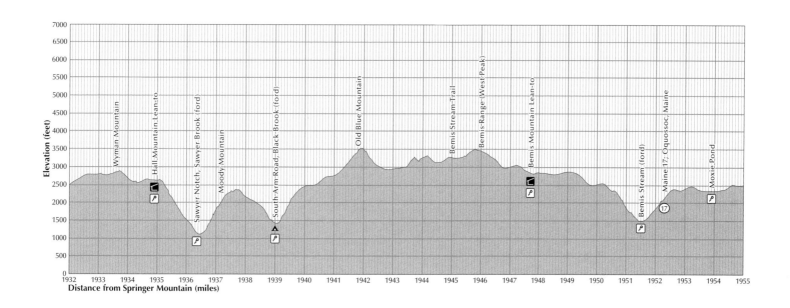

Elevation (feet)

7000
6500
6000
5500
5000
4500
4000
3500
3000
2500
2000
1500
1000
500
0

Wyman Mountain
Hall Mountain Lean-to
Sawyer Notch, Sawyer Brook (ford)
Moody Mountain
South Arm Road; Black Brook (ford)
Old Blue Mountain
Bemis Stream Trail
Bemis Range (West Peak)
Bemis Mountain Lean-to
Bemis Stream (ford)
Maine 17; Oquossoc, Maine
Moxie Pond

1932 1933 1934 1935 1936 1937 1938 1939 1940 1941 1942 1943 1944 1945 1946 1947 1948 1949 1950 1951 1952 1953 1954 1955

Distance from Springer Mountain (miles)

MAINE

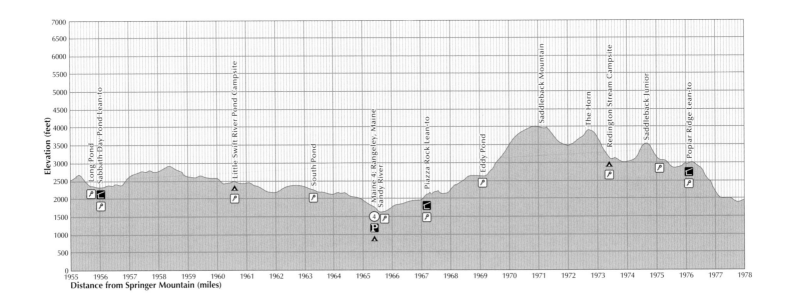

Elevation (feet)

Distance from Springer Mountain (miles)

Long Pond
Sabbath Day Pond Lean-to
Little Swift River Pond Campsite
South Pond
Maine 4: Rangeley, Maine
Sandy River
Piazza Rock Lean-to
Eddy Pond
Saddleback Mountain
The Horn
Redington Stream Campsite
Saddleback Junior
Poplar Ridge Lean-to

Appalachian Trail Book of Profiles

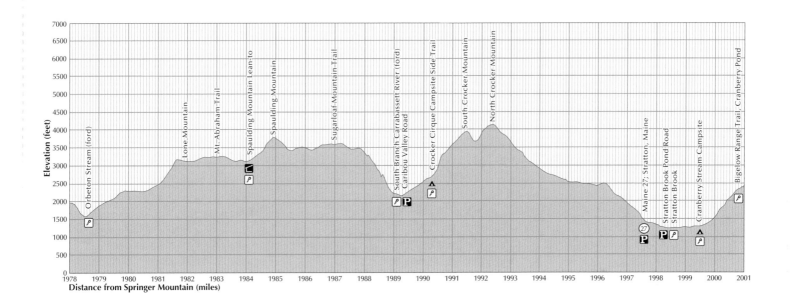

Elevation (feet)

7000
6500
6000
5500
5000
4500
4000
3500
3000
2500
2000
1500
1000
500
0

Orbeton Stream (ford)

Lone Mountain

Mt. Abraham Trail

Spaulding Mountain Lean-to

Spaulding Mountain

Sugarloaf Mountain Trail

South Branch Carrabassett River (ford)
Caribou Valley Road

Crocker Cirque Campsite Side Trail

South Crocker Mountain

North Crocker Mountain

Maine 27; Stratton, Maine

Stratton Brook Pond Road
Stratton Brook

Cranberry Stream Campsite

Bigelow Range Trail, Cranberry Pond

1978 1979 1980 1981 1982 1983 1984 1985 1986 1987 1988 1989 1990 1991 1992 1993 1994 1995 1996 1997 1998 1999 2000 2001

Distance from Springer Mountain (miles)

MAINE

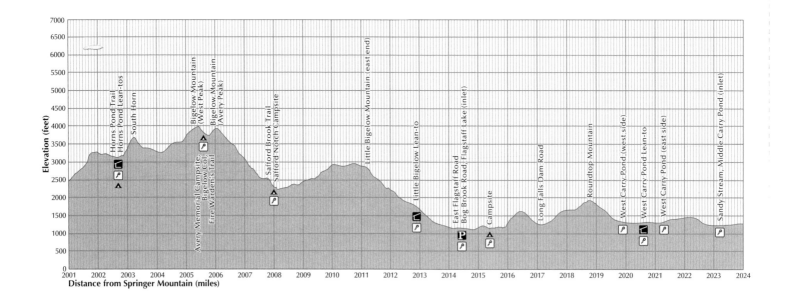

Elevation (feet)

7000
6500
6000
5500
5000
4500
4000
3500
3000
2500
2000
1500
1000
500
0

Horns Pond Trail
Horns Pond Lean-tos

South Horn

Bigelow Mountain (West Peak)

Bigelow Mountain (Avery Peak)

Avery Memorial Campsite, Bigelow Col, Fire Warden's Trail

Safford Brook Trail

Safford Notch Campsite

Little Bigelow Mountain (east end)

Little Bigelow Lean-to

East Flagstaff Road

Bog Brook Road, Flagstaff Lake (inlet)

Campsite

Long Falls Dam Road

Roundtop Mountain

West Carry Pond (west side)

West Carry Pond Lean-to

West Carry Pond (east side)

Sandy Stream, Middle Carry Pond (inlet)

Distance from Springer Mountain (miles)

2001 2002 2003 2004 2005 2006 2007 2008 2009 2010 2011 2012 2013 2014 2015 2016 2017 2018 2019 2020 2021 2022 2023 2024

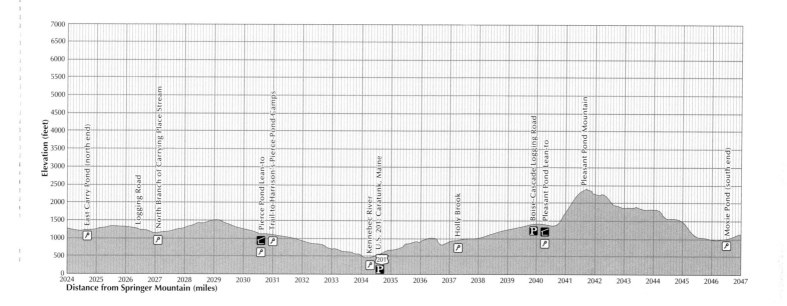

Elevation (feet)

7000
6500
6000
5500
5000
4500
4000
3500
3000
2500
2000
1500
1000
500
0

East Carry Pond (north end)

Logging Road

North Branch of Carrying Place Stream

Pierce Pond Lean-to

Trail-to-Harrison's-Pierce-Pond-Camps

Kennebec River

U.S. 201; Caratunk, Maine

Holly Brook

Boise-Cascade Logging Road

Pleasant Pond Lean-to

Pleasant Pond Mountain

Moxie Pond (south end)

2024 2025 2026 2027 2028 2029 2030 2031 2032 2033 2034 2035 2036 2037 2038 2039 2040 2041 2042 2043 2044 2045 2046 2047

Distance from Springer Mountain (miles)

MAINE

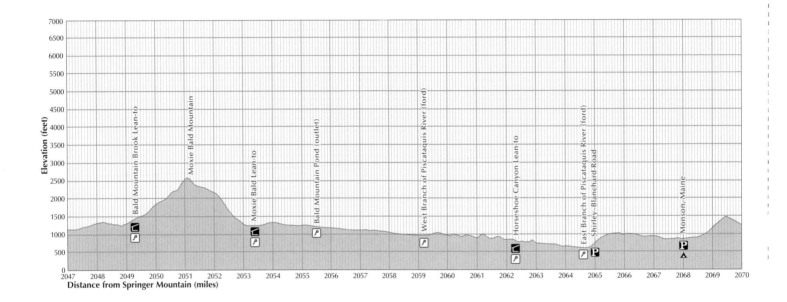

Elevation (feet) — vertical axis: 0, 500, 1000, 1500, 2000, 2500, 3000, 3500, 4000, 4500, 5000, 5500, 6000, 6500, 7000

Labels (left to right):
- Bald Mountain Brook Lean-to
- Moxie Bald Mountain
- Moxie Bald Lean-to
- Bald Mountain Pond (outlet)
- West Branch of Piscataquis River (ford)
- Horseshoe Canyon Lean-to
- East Branch of Piscataquis River (ford)
- Shirley–Blanchard Road
- Monson–Maine

Distance from Springer Mountain (miles)

2047 2048 2049 2050 2051 2052 2053 2054 2055 2056 2057 2058 2059 2060 2061 2062 2063 2064 2065 2066 2067 2068 2069 2070

Elevation (feet)

7000
6500
6000
5500
5000
4500
4000
3500
3000
2500
2000
1500
1000
500
0

Maine 15
Spectacle Pond (outlet)
Bell Pond
Lily Pond
Leeman Brook Lean-to
North Pond (outlet)
Little Wilson Falls
Little Wilson Stream
Big-Wilson-Stream-(ford)
Montreal, Maine & Atlantic Railroad
Wilson Valley Lean-to
Long Pond Stream (ford)
Long Pond Stream Lean-to
Barren Mountain
Cloud Pond Lean-to Side Trail
Fourth Mountain

2070 2071 2072 2073 2074 2075 2076 2077 2078 2079 2080 2081 2082 2083 2084 2085 2086 2087 2088 2089 2090 2091 2092 2093

Distance from Springer Mountain (miles)

MAINE

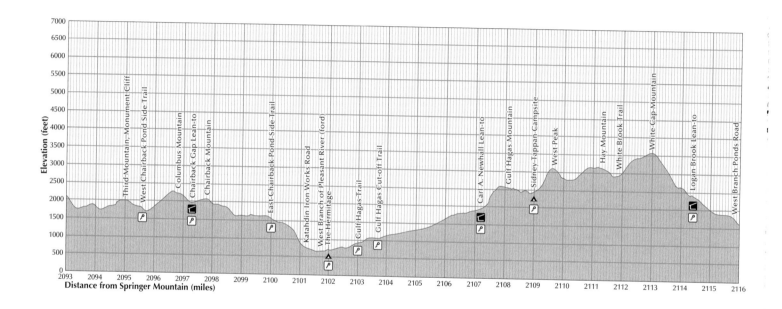

Elevation (feet)

Distance from Springer Mountain (miles)

Labels (left to right):
- Third Mountain–Monument Cliff
- West Chairback Pond Side Trail
- Columbus Mountain
- Chairback Gap Lean-to
- Chairback Mountain
- East-Chairback-Pond-Side-Trail
- Katahdin Iron Works Road
- West Branch of Pleasant River (ford)
- The Hermitage
- Gulf Hagas Trail
- Gulf Hagas Cut-off Trail
- Carl A. Newhall Lean-to
- Gulf Hagas Mountain
- Sidney-Tappan-Campsite
- West Peak
- Hay Mountain
- White Brook Trail
- White-Cap-Mountain
- Logan Brook lean-to
- West Branch Ponds Road

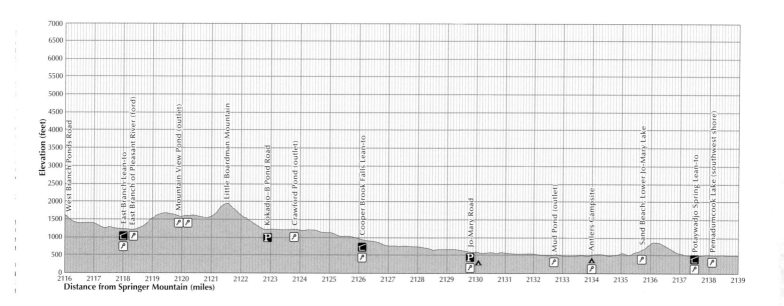

Elevation (feet)

7000
6500
6000
5500
5000
4500
4000
3500
3000
2500
2000
1500
1000
500
0

West Branch Ponds Road

East Branch Lean-to
East Branch of Pleasant River (ford)

Mountain View Pond (outlet)

Little Boardman Mountain

Kokadjo–B Pond Road

Crawford Pond (outlet)

Cooper Brook Falls Lean-to

Jo-Mary Road

Mud Pond (outlet)

Antlers Campsite

Sand Beach, Lower Jo-Mary Lake

Potaywadjo Spring Lean-to

Pemadumcook Lake (southwest shore)

2116 2117 2118 2119 2120 2121 2122 2123 2124 2125 2126 2127 2128 2129 2130 2131 2132 2133 2134 2135 2136 2137 2138 2139

Distance from Springer Mountain (miles)

MAINE

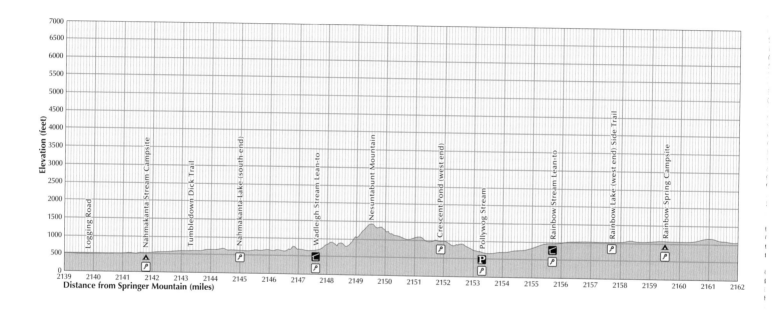

Elevation (feet)

7000
6500
6000
5500
5000
4500
4000
3500
3000
2500
2000
1500
1000
500
0

Logging Road

Nahmakanta Stream Campsite

Tumbledown Dick Trail

Nahmakanta Lake (south end)

Wadleigh Stream Lean-to

Nesuntabunt Mountain

Crescent Pond (west end)

Pollywog Stream

Rainbow Stream Lean-to

Rainbow Lake (west end) Side Trail

Rainbow Spring Campsite

Distance from Springer Mountain (miles)

2139 2140 2141 2142 2143 2144 2145 2146 2147 2148 2149 2150 2151 2152 2153 2154 2155 2156 2157 2158 2159 2160 2161 2162

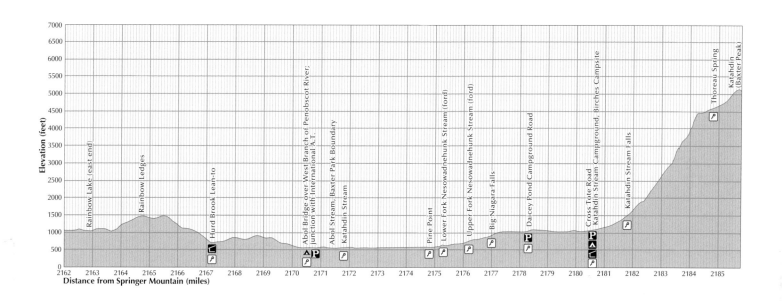

Distance from Springer Mountain (miles)

Elevation (feet)

Want maps with that?

Every official Appalachian Trail guide referenced in this book includes a volunteer-generated guidebook and four to seven maps with profiles such as these—maps that show you where you are in terms of the trail corridor, federal or state ownership of these public lands, and your relationship to the world just beyond the corridor. They are essential to your safety, in case you need to leave (or send a buddy) for help in a hurry. They also make your visit more enjoyable by enhancing the sense of place, as the guidebooks do with detailed footpath descriptions and background on landmarks: what went on there before the A.T. existed. Except for Maine, maps are available for purchase separately, some as sets, some individually.

These official guides can be purchased directly from the Appalachian Trail Conservancy's *Ultimate Appalachian Trail Store*® by visiting <www.atctrailstore.org> (QR code below right) or by calling toll-free to (888) 287-8673 on nonholiday weekdays between 9 a.m. and 4:30 p.m. Eastern time:

> *Appalachian Trail Guide to Maine*
> *Appalachian Trail Guide to New Hampshire–Vermont*
> *Appalachian Trail Guide to Massachusetts–Connecticut*
> *Appalachian Trail Guide to New York–New Jersey*
> *Appalachian Trail Guide to Pennsylvania*
> *Appalachian Trail Guide to Maryland and Northern Virginia*
> *Appalachian Trail Guide to Shenandoah National Park*
> *Appalachian Trail Guide to Central Virginia*
> *Appalachian Trail Guide to Southwest Virginia*
> *Appalachian Trail Guide to Tennessee–North Carolina**
> *Appalachian Trail Guide to North Carolina–Georgia**

* Includes Great Smoky Mountains National Park

Protect, enhance, and promote the Trail experience: That's what ATC does.

You can help by joining the
Appalachian Trail Conservancy today!

You can become a member by going to
www.appalachiantrail.org/join
or calling
(304) 535-6331